The Complete Guide to

Portuguese Water Dogs

Jordan Honeycutt

Publication Data

Jordan Honeycutt
The Complete Guide to Portuguese Water Dogs – First edition.
Summary: "Successfully raising a Portuguese Water Dog from puppy to old age"
Provided by publisher.
ISBN: 978-1-954288-81-2
[1. The Complete Guide to Portuguese Water Dogs – Non-Fiction] I. Title.

Design by Sorin Rădulescu
First paperback edition, 2023

TABLE OF CONTENTS

Chapter 1

Chapter 2

Chapter 6

Potty Training Your Portuguese Water Dog 57

Chapter 7

Socializing Your Portuguese Water Dog 67

Chapter 14

Chapter 15

CHAPTER 1

Breed History

What is a Portuguese Water Dog?

> *The PWD is an active, energetic, intelligent breed. They require daily exercise, such as long walks, playing Frisbee or fetch, hiking, or swimming. Mental stimulation in the form of training is very important in the first year. This breed has a true need to be an active member of the family. The PWD does not thrive in a home that is sedentary. A family that leads an active lifestyle and enjoys having their dog tag along makes the best PWD home.*
>
> JILL ROUDEBUSH
> *Maritimo Portuguese Water Dogs*

The Portuguese Water Dog is a head-turner with its medium-to-large muscular body covered in soft black, brown, or white curls. Affectionately referred to as Porties, this breed, which was once almost extinct, has found favor in recent years and has climbed up to number 44 on the list of top breeds, according to the American Kennel Club (AKC). Bred to work on fishermen's boats, this breed is as intelligent and hardworking as it is adorable, and these dogs love to be around their people.

Photo Courtesy of
Marina Shenton

History of the Portuguese Water Dog

According to the AKC, the Portuguese Water Dog has several possible origins. One commonly accepted theory dates all the way back to 200 BC on the Iberian Peninsula, now known as the areas of Gibraltar, Andorra, Spain, and Portugal. Over time, this region was invaded by several foreign groups, including the Romans, Visigoths, and Moors, who all brought their own dogs to the land. As these strong, muscular working dogs began to breed with each other, a new breed eventually emerged.

The resulting breed was a strong, hardworking dog that was willing to work in and out of the water. It is thought that fishermen at the time saw the value these dogs brought to their work and claimed them as "fishermen's dogs." This is the dog that is now known as the Portuguese Water Dog.

Another theory claims the breed originated near the border between Russia and China as early as 700 BC. These dogs were originally bred as herding dogs, but there is speculation that some of the dogs were captured by nomadic Berber warriors who then took the dogs across Asia to North Africa. Eventually, the dogs were brought to the Iberian Peninsula by the Moors, who were descendants of the Berber warriors, and the dogs found favor with the fishermen.

There is yet another similar theory that claims the dogs originated in Asia, traveling with another nomadic tribe that came from Germany, the Goths. As a segment of the group called the Ostrogoths headed west, their dogs became what is known as the poodle today. Another element of the Goths, the Visigoths, traveled south and eventually reached the Iberian Peninsula.

Regardless of exact origin, the Portuguese Water Dog did eventually make its way to the Iberian Peninsula, where the dogs put their strength and keen water skills to good use. The breed could be found carrying messages from boat to boat or boat to shore, retrieving tackle, and even herding fish into nets.

> **"**
> *Because these dogs were bred to work on fishing boats with their owners, this breed is very people-oriented.*
>
> CHERYL W. HOOFNAGLE
> *Blue Run Portuguese Water Dogs*
> **"**

Modern History

As time went on and fishing boats became more modern, the Portuguese Water Dog found its numbers decreasing, and the breed was on the verge of extinction. It wasn't until the 1930s when Vasco Bensaude, a wealthy Portuguese businessman, was reportedly captivated by the dogs and began the work to revive the breed. He began seeking out the first dogs for his kennel, which he called Algarbiorum. Though there were not many of these dogs still working the fishing boats, Bensaude acquired a male and a female and then eventually acquired Leao, the male that would become the foundation and set the standard for the entire breed.

Bensaude bred these dogs for 30 years but did not regularly sell them. Instead, he gifted the dogs to friends and colleagues. When Bensaude died in 1957, his widow gave the dogs in the kennel to a friend, who eventually gave a Portuguese water dog to an American couple from Connecticut, Mr. and Mrs. Herbert Miller, thus introducing what would become the first breeding stock in the United States.

About a year later, the Millers acquired a male and bred their first litter of Portuguese Water Dogs in 1971. A year after that, the Millers established the Portuguese Water Dog Club of America at a gathering with only 14 other people. Their litter of the previous year became the first officially recorded litter of the club.

It wasn't until 1984 that the Portuguese Water Dog became eligible for AKC registration in the working class. Now, after nearly disappearing from the fishing boats off the Iberian Peninsula, the Portuguese Water Dog has made a comeback and climbed its way up the charts of most popular dog breeds in America.

Popular Culture

The Portuguese Water Dog was most recently made famous by the Obama family when a special Portie, Bo, was welcomed into the White House in 2009. Bo was a gift to the Obama family by Senator Ted Kennedy, one Barack Obama claimed his girls well-deserved after living through the campaign. Four years later, the Obamas welcomed a second Portuguese Water Dog to the White House named Sunny.

Physical Characteristics

The Portuguese Water Dog is a medium-to-large dog weighing anywhere from 35 to 60 pounds on average. It is a sturdy and well-built dog, bred to work alongside fishermen in and out of the water, and is the picture of soundness. This breed is powerful and muscular, with solid bone structure and a characteristically large but proportional head. Their water-repellant coats come in two types, curly and wavy, and their

Photo Courtesy of Nancy Puskorius

feet are webbed, making them excellent divers and swimmers.

Male Porties should stand 20 to 23 inches tall at the withers, and females 17 to 21 inches. These dogs are slightly longer than they are tall, and they possess a broad and deep chest that drops down to the elbows, with long ribs that allow for greater lung capacity.

According to the AKC breed standard, a Portuguese Water Dog should have a steady, penetrating, and attentive expression with dark eyes that are set well apart, roundish, and neither prominent nor sunken.

FUN FACT

Portuguese Water Dog Club of America (PWDCA)

The Portuguese Water Dog Club of America (PWDCA) is the American Kennel Club (AKC) parent club for this breed in the United States. Founded in 1972 by a group of 16 Portuguese Water Dog enthusiasts in New Canaan, CT, the club now boasts nearly 1,600 members. Today, the PWDCA publishes an award-winning breed magazine and offers several unique award categories for members. For more information about this group, visit www.pwdca.org.

A Portuguese Water Dog's ears should be heart-shaped, set above the eye line, and not reach below the jaw, and his muzzle should be substantial but wider at the base than the nose. His tail should be thick at the base and carried gallantly or used purposefully as a rudder.

Coat Types

The Portuguese Water Dog possesses a single coat of thick hair that presents in two acceptable ways. Curly coats present in compact, somewhat dull curls. Wavy coats present in a much looser, falling wave rather than a tight curl. Either coat type is acceptable, according to the AKC breed standard.

Along with the two hair types seen among Portuguese Water Dogs, several color combinations occur. While black is the most common color for a Portie, this breed can also be seen in various shades of brown, white, or a combination of black or brown and white.

Typical Breed Behavior

> "
> *PWDs are 'Velcro' dogs and need your time and attention. They do not do well alone.*
>
> MARLENE NICEWANDER
> *Cove's End Portuguese Water Dogs*
> "

According to the breed standard, the Portuguese Water Dog should be "an animal of spirited disposition, self-willed, brave, and very resistant to fatigue. A dog of exceptional intelligence and a loyal companion, it obeys its master with facility and apparent pleasure. It is obedient with those who look after it or with those for whom it works."

Because this breed was bred to work enthusiastically alongside a master, the dogs are naturally energetic. Proper training can go a long way to control the energy of a healthy Portie, but physical and mental exercise requirements remain high. While they make wonderfully happy companions, they are workers by nature and will not be content as house pets without a job to accomplish.

Is a Portuguese Water Dog Right for You?

As previously discussed, the Portuguese Water Dog makes an excellent and obedient companion in the proper setting. If you are looking for a dog that is willing to work or play alongside you day in and day out, this breed may be just what you are looking for. However, if you are looking for a house dog to be a companion at a slower pace of life, the Portuguese Water Dog may be too much for you.

According to Christie Kello with Windward Portuguese Water Dogs, "The best-suited home for a Portuguese Water Dog is an already active home. This is a working breed that requires daily physical and mental stimulation. They need to have time to chase a ball or play Frisbee, go for hikes to explore, and be challenged mentally. While many homes like to teach tricks, etc., they tend to not do enough physically with their [dog]. Homes that are already active, such as avid hikers or joggers, are great because they are already committed to physical activity. This is not the breed for a family that wants a dog [that] can go for a walk once a week and will otherwise lie around. That's not what they were bred for. While they do enjoy a good cuddle while you watch a movie, that also needs to be balanced with exercise."

A Portie craves purpose and is driven to work, and he will not be content to lounge around for most of the day. If you are willing to put in the work and be a strong leader for a willing Portuguese Water Dog, he will reward you with loyalty and hard work for all your days together.

CHAPTER 2

Choosing Your Portuguese Water Dog

Buying vs. Adopting

Once you have decided that a Portuguese Water Dog is the right breed for you, you may be wondering where to begin your search for the perfect dog. The first decision you will have to make is whether you will purchase a Portuguese Water Dog from a breeder or adopt one from a rescue.

We are all touched by those videos of dogs in need, but often it isn't as simple as adopting a dog that needs a home. Often, dogs in a rescue organization have special medical or social needs and will require a unique owner to meet those needs. If you can provide the patience and care it may take to adopt a rescue Portuguese Water Dog, please do! The bond between a rescued dog and its owner can be just as strong as the bond you form with a new pup.

One benefit of adopting a Portuguese Water Dog is having the opportunity to know its personality before you bring the dog home. You will likely know ahead of time if the dog is good with children or not, if it has any behavioral or aggression issues, and what its level of energy may be. As long as you ask the right questions, there should be very few surprises when adopting a mature Portuguese Water Dog.

The Differences Between Animal Shelters and Rescue Organizations

In the United States, there are three classifications for pet and animal rescues: municipal shelters, no-kill shelters, and nonprofit rescues. In this section, we will outline the key differences between them.

Municipal Shelters

Municipal shelters are funded and run by local governments. These shelters take in stray animals and animals abandoned or surrendered by their owners. Animals are given a limited amount of time to be adopted before they may be euthanized due to a lack of space for more incoming animals.

Municipal shelters house their animals in a kennel-like setting in one centralized location. Many have veterinarians on staff to provide basic

care and sterilization. While most have a small paid staff to care for the animals, many facilities rely on volunteers to help attend to the animals and clean kennels. Adoption fees are usually lowest at municipal shelters, and nearly all require an animal to be spayed or neutered before leaving the shelter.

While shelters are an excellent way to find local pets in need, you likely won't find a purebred Portuguese Water Dog in the shelter. However, you may find a mixed-breed dog that meets your qualifications. Municipal shelters are almost always fighting an overpopulation problem. Be aware that if you choose to adopt from a municipal shelter, it isn't uncommon for even a non-aggressive dog to act fearful or show aggression when in a stressful environment such as a shelter. This phenomenon is called "kennel syndrome," and it can sadly keep some good dogs from being adopted. Ask if your shelter allows a trial period where you can take the dog home for a few days to see if he is a good fit for your family. This will give you the opportunity to see his personality shine outside of the high-stress kennel environment.

No-Kill Shelter

A no-kill shelter will only accept as many animals as it can handle. These shelters will not euthanize a dog due to lack of space, but they will turn dogs away. Many dogs find themselves at a no-kill shelter for an extended period of time, months, and sometimes even years, before they are adopted.

Some no-kill shelters have a central location with kennels to house the animals, but many often utilize foster homes for animals as well. These homes allow the dogs to live a more normal life while they are waiting for their forever families. Sometimes that is just what a dog with kennel syndrome needs to become more adoptable.

Nonprofit Rescue

These organizations are typically operated by a crew of volunteers and are privately funded or dependent on donations. These organizations will utilize foster homes for their animals, and many have no centralized facility at all. Private rescue organizations are often breed-specific, meaning they are dedicated to rescuing one dog type, such as the Portuguese Water Dog.

Because these nonprofit organizations typically do not have an on-staff veterinarian to care for the animals, they often must pay full price for services, which can become a significant expense. Due to these higher expenses, rescues typically have much higher adoption fees and adoption standards than shelters. Not only do many require a detailed application, some even require a home inspection before an adoption is approved.

Much like purchasing from a breeder, these private rescue organizations will often maintain contact with the adopter for several months to ensure

FUN FACT

Ancestral Lineage

According to one theory, the origins of this majestic dog may date back as far as 200 BC on the Iberian Peninsula. This theory, posited by former PWDCA president Maryanne Murray, claims that three ancient dog breeds owned by the Romans, Visigoths, and Moors interbred and produced the Portuguese Water Dog of today. Others argue that the most likely ancestors of the PWD include the Poodle, Irish Water Spaniel, and Kerry Blue Terrier.

the placement is going well and may even do a follow-up home visit. Many also have policies in place mandating that a dog be returned to them if the adopter is no longer able to care for him for any reason.

Tips for Adoption

Many animals are homeless through no fault of their own. Unfortunate circumstances can find any dog in a situation without a loving place to go home to. While we have already discussed the potential behavioral or medical needs of a rescue dog, not all dogs in need of a home have these special needs. Perhaps a family is forced to move and is unable to take the dog along, or a death leaves the dog without his owner or home. Dogs in these situations are often highly adoptable and will adjust easily to a new home.

If you do choose to adopt a rescue Portuguese Water Dog rather than purchase from a breeder, reach out to all your local shelters and let them know what you are looking for. While chances are slim that you'll find a Portie in a local shelter, it doesn't hurt to have them keep an eye out just in case.

Another good place to begin your rescue search is through a local breeder. Find a Portuguese Water Dog breeder near your area and ask them if they have any information on local rescues. If not, take your search online. If you feel called to rescue a Portuguese Water Dog in need, seek out a reputable organization quickly, as many breed-specific rescues have waiting lists for available dogs. Don't hesitate to get your application in if you see a dog you're interested in!

Breeder Reputation

If, instead of adoption, you decide to seek a Portuguese Water Dog from a breeder, it is imperative that you choose a reputable breeder with ample experience. With so many people flippantly breeding dogs from their homes these days, it can be challenging to know who to trust. There is a significant difference between a breeder who is breeding for the sole purpose of profit and one who is dedicated to the betterment of the breed.

One significant difference between a responsible breeder and one who is not is that "backyard breeders" are rarely doing the testing required to ensure the health of their litters. Some even turn out to be puppy mills, a place where dogs are kept alive to do little more than pump out litter after litter for profit. Often, dogs in puppy mills are kept in small cages in unclean conditions.

A reputable and responsible Portuguese Water Dog breeder will be regarded as such among the Portie community. If you find a good breeder without a litter available, ask them for references to other good breeders.

Finding a Breeder

"

It's best to buy from a local breeder where you can meet the dam, interview the breeder, and be certain you are dealing with a person who does all the appropriate health testing on the sire and dam. Breeders who compete their dogs in conformation and who belong to the Portuguese Water Dog Club of America are likely to be breeding to preserve the character of the breed, as opposed to breeding just to supply pets to the pet market. Look for a breeder who follows the health of the dogs they have produced for the life of the dog.

CHERYL W. HOOFNAGLE
Blue Run Portuguese Water Dogs

"

It is both easier and also more challenging to find a reputable Portuguese Water Dog breeder with the help of the internet. While a quick search online may bring up a plethora of options, not all of these options will be good, reputable breeders. In order to determine the good breeders from someone who is just trying to make a quick buck, there are several questions you need to ask.

Can I Visit the Breeding Facility?

The answer to this question should always be a resounding yes. A breeder might not allow you into certain areas of the facility for the safety of the puppies. There is a concern about tracking in diseases that could be detrimental to a young puppy's undeveloped immune system. However, a quality breeder should always allow you to come on-site and see other dogs in their program. If they refuse, this could be a sign they have something to hide, and you should reconsider.

How Long Have You Been Breeding Portuguese Water Dogs?

You should only buy from an experienced breeder who is well established, so the answer to this question should be several years. A quality breeder who has several years of experience will know all the ins and outs of breeding for only the most desirable traits and healthy dogs.

Can I See Veterinary Records for Both Parents?

When investing your time and money into a Portuguese Water Dog puppy, you will want to have an open and transparent line of communication with your chosen breeder. If the breeder is not willing to share the medical records of the puppy's parents, this is a signal that you should find another breeder. Both the dam and the sire should have been checked by specialists and cleared for defects. The breeder should also provide proof of genetic testing.

Do You Ever Sell to a Broker or Pet Shop?

If the answer is yes, walk away from this breeder immediately and do not support them. A responsible breeder, breeding for the betterment of the dog's health and appearance, will never sell one of their animals to a broker or a pet store. Reputable breeders want to meet the families of each of their puppies to be sure they will be properly cared for. Puppies found in a pet shop are bred for profit alone and come with no health guarantee.

Health Tests and Certifications

> 66
>
> *Ask for proof of health testing! A vet's health clearance certificate is not adequate—that just means the puppy or dog is healthy at the moment. You need copies of those genetic certificates (eyes/heart/hips) that are current. No proof of genetic health testing? Stay away. And you can double-check that the information you've received is accurate by searching the sire's and dam's AKC registration numbers at the ofa.org site. Unfortunately, there have been breeders who've skewed certificates, or have had dogs pass an exam one year and fail later, and they've given you the old certification. Verify those certificates!*
>
> ROBIN L. BURMEISTER
> *Windward Portuguese Water Dogs*
>
> 99

There are numerous genetic conditions that Portuguese Water Dogs are prone to developing. Before agreeing to purchase a puppy, ask for a detailed list of the tests the breeder performed on the parents and ask for copies of the test results. These tests should be performed by certified specialists for each potential ailment, such as a board-certified veterinary cardiologist and ophthalmologist. Just because the breeder had the dogs checked out by a general veterinarian does not mean they were genetically tested for undesirable traits.

Breeder Contracts and Guarantees

A good breeder will always guarantee the health of their puppies. Look for guarantees or contracts that will refund most or all of the cost of the puppy in the event any congenital health conditions appear within the first year. Beware of breeders who only offer to replace the puppy with a healthy one, with no option to receive a refund instead. If the breeder produced a genetically unhealthy puppy the first time, why would you want to bring home another puppy from the same place? Many people are also unwilling to return their dog for a replacement, as they have already become attached. This is a low-risk guarantee from a breeder and may be a warning sign. On the other hand, a responsible breeder will always take back a dog that you can no longer care for, no matter the reason.

Many times, a breeder's health guarantee will have stipulations. These may include not neutering or spaying until after a year so that the dog's joints are allowed to fully develop, feeding your puppy a proper diet, and regular visits to the vet. As much as a responsible breeder wants their puppies to remain in perfect health for their entire life, not all owners care for a dog the same way, and health results will vary based on lifestyle.

Many Portie breeders also have a strict no-breeding policy and will include mandatory sterilization in their contract. If you plan to show your Portuguese Water Dog or breed the dog yourself, you will want to find a breeder that allows your dog to remain intact.

Remember, no matter how good the breeding lines are or how thorough the testing, no breeder can guarantee perfect health for a dog's entire life. If something does go wrong with your puppy, before putting the blame on the breeder, it is important to understand any role you may have unwittingly played in the situation.

Picking a Puppy

> *The best advice to give a potential owner is that you do not choose the puppy; trust your breeder to choose the right puppy for you. A responsible, reputable breeder will take the time to get to know you and your needs when it comes to adding a puppy to your home. With their breed knowledge and experience, they should be able to find the right puppy that will fit in your home. A good breeder will tell you 'no' when you have your heart set on a puppy that is clearly not going to be the right fit.*
>
> CHRISTIE KELLO
> *Windward Portuguese Water Dogs*

General temperament and behavior should remain relatively consistent in a litter of well-bred Portuguese Water Dogs and should align with the AKC's breed standard. However, individual puppy personalities will vary. If you are able, visit the breeding facility to pick out your new pup from the litter so you can get a better feel for his personality beforehand. If you are unable to visit the facility to choose your pup, let the breeder know what type of personality you would prefer and let them match you with a dog that fits within those standards. These breeders should know, in general, which puppies will be the most outgoing, which pups will be spunkier, which pups will tend to be more laid-back, and so on.

According to Jill Roudebush with Maritimo Portuguese Water Dogs in Ohio,

> **"**
>
> *"In order to place the right puppy in the right family, it is important to match the puppy's temperament to the family's lifestyle. It is also important to understand what the family's expectations are for their new puppy as well as the ages of each family member. While raising a litter, I pay close attention to how my puppies play and respond to each other. If I have an elderly couple, a family with small children, and a person who wants to do agility or water work, knowing how my puppies respond to their littermates will help me place them in the right home. A puppy that tends to go to a quiet corner when all the puppies are playing is best suited for a quieter home, such as an older couple with no children. The puppy that is high drive with lots of energy would be best for the person wanting to do agility or water work. The puppy that is the middle-of-the-road type would do well in a family with small children. Puppies that tend to hang out in a corner by themselves have the chance of being fear biters, which does not work in a home with small children. A puppy that has a lot of energy and drive is better in a working home and not one with children or a less active older couple."*
>
> **"**

Though puppies will vary in personality, none are better or worse than the other. You should, however, have a type of dog in mind that you are hoping for so that you and the breeder can make the best choice for your family and for your future puppy.

Raising Multiple Puppies from the Same Litter

Some people wish to purchase two puppies from the same litter and raise them together. If you are hoping for two Portuguese Water Dogs, this may seem like a good solution. However, be forewarned that raising two pups from the same litter can be a challenge. Not only are you doubling the work of raising a puppy, but each puppy will need independent, one-on-one training and attention, meaning you will be investing a great deal of time into your dogs individually until they are well-trained.

Not only can the attention requirements of two puppies become overwhelming, the bond the two littermates will form can actually eclipse the bond formed between dog and owner. If you wish to have an unbreakable bond with your dog, it is wise to only bring home one at a time so that those deep bonds can form. A reputable breeder should always advise against getting two dogs at once, and many breeders will refuse to sell multiples unless you have proof that you can care for them both properly.

If you really want to have two Portuguese Water Dogs, get them at different times. Establish a bond with one dog and then get another and do the same before the two are allowed to pair up. While it may seem impossible, do this by intentionally spending quality alone time with your new dog as often as possible. No matter how intentional you are, however, many find that the two dogs will develop a bond that could potentially take away from the one shared between human and dog.

CHAPTER 3

Preparing for Your Portuguese Water Dog

I t is important to prepare your home and family before you bring home your Portuguese Water Dog. Puppy pick-up day is exciting for all, but it can quickly turn stressful if you realize you aren't quite prepared for your new arrival after all. Taking the time to get everything ready and in order before you bring home your Portie can help your first few days together go much smoother.

Preparing Children and other Pets

Whether you have children or other fur children, it's important you prepare everyone ahead of time for your fluffy new arrival. As can be expected, both children and other pets will need to adjust to the new changes in the home. You will need to be patient with all involved until everyone has settled into a new normal routine.

Because most children are typically excited to bring home a new puppy, adjusting them to the idea will likely be easy. The most important aspect of preparing your children is teaching them how to safely handle and care for the pup. A small child can unintentionally harm a young Portie simply by trying to show affection in a manner that is a little too rough. Also, puppy teeth are sharp, and your small pup can also unintentionally hurt your child by trying to play. Because of this, you should carefully supervise interactions between children and the puppy, even if you think your children understand.

Adjusting current pets to a new Portuguese Water Dog can be a little more challenging. Depending on your current pet's personality, transitioning a new puppy into the family may be easy, or it may take some work. Either way, begin warming your current pets up before puppy pick-up day so they aren't overwhelmed by the new "intruder."

Talk to your chosen breeder and ask if they will allow you to take home a toy or a blanket with your new Portie's scent on it before bringing home the puppy. This may require you to drop off a toy or blanket to get his scent on it, so make sure you ask in plenty of time before the big day. Introduce this scent to your current pets several days before you bring home your dog so they can get used to it.

When you do bring your Portuguese Water Dog home, you will need to be careful with the first introductions. If possible, have someone help you

Photo Courtesy of
Chris and Jon Zombek

so that there is an extra set of hands around in case you need them. Always begin introductions in a neutral area where your current dogs are less likely to become territorial. However, for safety reasons, this neutral area should not be a public park or anywhere else other dogs frequent because this may put your unvaccinated pup at risk. Instead, choose an unused area of the yard around your home or the home of a friend or family member.

Keep the first meeting brief so that no one is overwhelmed. All dogs should be leashed with a bit of slack so they can safely greet the new addition. After seeing first reactions, use your judgment and slowly give them more freedom to get acquainted as you see fit. Remember, stop all interactions and separate the dogs before any parties become overwhelmed or stressed.

Jill Roudebush from Maritimo Portuguese Water Dogs in Ohio says, "It is important to remember that when you pick your new puppy up, it will be stressed for the first few days. Be sure not to overwhelm it with too many new people or visiting pets. Allow the puppy to adjust to its new home and family first."

If the interactions between your existing dogs and your new puppy aren't going as well as you'd hoped, you may need to take more extreme, slow measures. If this is the case, try separating your dogs in separate rooms but close enough that they can smell and hear each other. Make sure you do not keep your current dogs out of a space they usually have, as this may cause jealousy issues. Again, use your judgment and allow the dogs more freedom with each other as you see progress. It may take a great deal of patience, but usually, dogs will become acclimated to each other and form a bond of their own that will become unbreakable.

If you are introducing your new puppy to a resident cat, keep both your cat and puppy safe by maintaining control of your puppy or by allowing them to meet while one animal is contained in a crate or separated by another barrier. Allow them short, controlled interactions at quiet moments of the day until they are both calm around each other. Always make sure your cat has a safe place to retreat to, preferably off the ground, such as a cat tower. Never force your cat to interact with your new puppy.

While a new Portuguese Water Dog is exciting, it can unintentionally become the focal point of life for a while. After all, puppies are much like babies! Remember to show your other dogs and pets some extra attention and love, so they know that they are still important members of the family and will not be forgotten. This can go a long way in helping everyone acclimate to the new addition with a good attitude.

Puppy-Proofing Your Home

> *I always recommend choosing an area of the house where the puppy will be allowed to hang out with the family. Gate that area off from the rest of the house and puppy-proof it. You will need to be sure that all electrical cords are out of reach; that there are no toxic plants, medicines, or chemicals in the area; and that any valuables are moved. The most important thing is to be there to monitor your puppy's free time, so that you can effectively teach it what is off-limits from the very beginning.*
>
> JILL ROUDEBUSH
> *Maritimo Portuguese Water Dogs*

Puppy-proofing your home is an essential task you must complete before your Portuguese Water Dog comes home with you. Although he may be small and cute, your Portuguese Water Dog pup may quickly find himself in things he shouldn't be if you don't prepare ahead of time. There are many seemingly harmless things in any home that can pose a danger to a curious puppy.

Tuck Away or Remove Electrical Cords Within the Puppy's Reach.

Even the most docile puppy may be enticed by the allure of an electrical cord. It is imperative you remove all cords from his reach to protect him from this hazard. If you cannot remove the cords from your puppy's reach, you may want to invest in some cord protectors. These cord wraps usually come infused with bitter flavors to help deter your Portie from chewing. If you find you have a particularly stubborn chewer, you can spritz the cords with hot pepper spray.

Invest in Fully Enclosed Trash Cans if You Do Not Have Them Already.

Do this for the kitchen trash can and the smaller bathroom and office trash cans too. While the paper in your office trash may not pose much danger, it will be a mess after it's been shredded by puppy teeth!

Lock Away all Drugs, Chemicals, and Cleaning Supplies.

If you tend to keep any medications in an area that your puppy may be able to reach, be sure to move those to a higher location, such as a dedicated, locked medicine cabinet. Puppies explore with their mouths, and snatching a bottle or box of medication off the sofa table could prove to be fatal for your new puppy.

Also, move any chemicals, cleaning supplies, dish pods, or laundry detergents into an enclosed area out of reach of your puppy. This includes any rat bait or poisons that your new puppy may find enticing. Even if these items are in an area of the house where your puppy will not be allowed, it only takes one curious adventure for your new Portuguese Water Dog to encounter something that could be harmful to him.

Remove Poisonous Houseplants.

If you don't already have pets in the house, you may not be aware that many houseplants are actually poisonous to dogs. Even some of the most common plants can be dangerous for a curious nibbling puppy. Some of the most common houseplants that are potentially dangerous for your new puppy are the corn plant, sago palm, aloe, and jade plant. There are many more common household plants that are poisonous to your dog. To find a complete list, visit the ASPCA website.

Don't worry; if you have one of the plants on this list, you don't have to give it up. Find a place that you are certain is out of reach from your puppy and leave it there. Houseplants are a wonderful addition to the home and provide health benefits for you and your puppy. As long as you are aware of the dangers and plan accordingly, your pup should remain safe.

Beware of Xylitol.

Xylitol is considered a sugar alcohol and is commonly found in items throughout almost every household. As people become more and more aware of the dangers of added sugars, companies are turning to xylitol, an additive that tastes sweet but does not spike blood sugar and insulin levels like sugar. Xylitol can be found in almost anything, but it is commonly found in chewing gum, mints, candies, toothpaste, and even peanut butter. Xylitol is highly toxic to dogs and can cause dangerously low blood sugar levels, resulting in weakness, seizures, trembling, or even death. When dogs consume very high levels of xylitol, it may cause necrosis of the liver, which often leads to death.

Be sure to keep all purses and bags, which may contain gum, candies, or toothpaste, out of reach of your puppy at all times. Have a designated area for guests' bags so that they are not accidentally left within reach. Also, check all food labels for xylitol. The use of peanut butter is often recommended to give a dog medication, but be sure to check that your peanut butter does not contain xylitol first.

Keep the Batteries Away.

While you probably don't have random batteries lying around on the floor, you may have remotes or small electronic toys. If your puppy can get hold of a battery-operated remote or toy, he can chew them to expose the battery. Small-button cell batteries are the most dangerous, as they are small enough for your puppy to swallow. Swallowing a battery is a serious, life-threatening issue and can cause internal burns. Call the nearest emergency vet immediately if you suspect your puppy may have swallowed a battery.

Put Away any Children's Toys.

Children's toys are often made up of small pieces that are a choking hazard to your dog. Be especially careful with toys that contain magnets inside, as these pose an extra risk of internal damage when more than one is consumed.

Keep Toilets Closed.

Many people use automatically refreshing toilet bowl cleaners attached to the bowl of their toilet. These can pose risks to a thirsty pup. Remove chemical cleaners from your toilet bowl, or make sure you always keep the lid down.

Set Up Puppy Gates.

After you have puppy-proofed your entire house, designate a safe common area of the house for your puppy to stay. Use puppy gates to block any doorways or staircases so that it will be easier for you to keep a close eye on your new Portuguese Water Dog. Having already puppy-proofed the entire house, you can be sure that even if your dog makes a great escape into a room where he is not allowed, the dangerous items have all been removed.

Accidents happen frequently because it only takes a second for a bored puppy to get into mischief. Preparation ahead of time is the key to avoiding these incidents and keeping your Portie safe.

Dangerous Things Your Dog Might Eat

It's nearly impossible to resist a sweet Portuguese Water Dog face staring up at you at the dinner table, begging for a bite. Although not recommended, if you get the urge to toss your Portie a bite to eat off your plate, you need to know ahead of time what he can safely have and what may pose a threat. There are several foods that, though harmless to humans, can cause illness or toxicity in dogs.

Chocolate

A favorite among humans, it is well-known chocolate can cause major issues for dogs. Chocolate contains methylxanthine, a stimulant that can stop a dog's metabolic process. Methylxanthines are found in especially high amounts in pure dark chocolate and baker's chocolate. Too much methylxanthine causes seizures and irregular heart function, which can lead to death.

Xylitol

As discussed above, xylitol is particularly dangerous to dogs as it does not take much to cause a dangerous or deadly reaction. Vomiting is typically the initial symptom of xylitol poisoning. If you suspect there is a chance your dog has ingested even a small amount of xylitol, call the veterinarian immediately because time is critical.

Raw or Cooked Bones

Raw or cooked bones are a choking hazard for your dog. The bones can break or splinter and become lodged in, or worse, puncture the digestive tract. This is especially true with cooked bones of any kind, as they become dry and brittle. Pork and poultry bones are especially dangerous as they are more likely to splinter and cause issues.

Though controversial, some veterinarians say that raw bones of the right variety can provide healthy nutrients and help prevent tartar and plaque buildup in the mouth. These bones are recommended only under very close supervision and only for a few minutes at a time, keeping the bone in the refrigerator for a maximum of four days before discarding. If the bone is breaking or if your dog seems to be swallowing any pieces, discard the bone immediately. If you prefer to skip the risk, look for bones in the pet store that are meant to withstand heavy chewing.

Other foods that may cause gastrointestinal upset or injury to your dog are grapes and raisins; certain nuts, including macadamia nuts; avocados, apple cores, and seeds; and anything in the allium family, including onions and garlic. This is not a comprehensive list, so it is best to check with your veterinarian before giving anything from your plate to your dog.

Supplies to Buy Ahead of Time

> **"**
>
> *I strongly encourage all of my puppy buyers to purchase at least one, if not two, crates. I always suggest a crate in the main family area and one in the bedroom. The PWD wants to be where you are.*
>
> PATTI MCKNIGHT
>
> *McKnight's PWDs*
>
> **"**

We've already discussed the importance of preparing for your Portuguese Water Dog ahead of time, and a large part of that is having all the supplies he will need ready to use before he arrives. However, with so many options out there, it can be difficult to know what you need and

what you may not need. This list of essentials will help you prepare for your pup and help your first few days together go smoothly.

Food and Water Bowls

Any walk down the food and water bowl aisle in a pet store can leave you confused and overwhelmed by all the options. There are different shapes, colors, sizes, and even materials. Some are ceramic, some metal, and some plastic. While it may be overwhelming, there are a few things to keep in mind to help you make the right decision for your Portie.

While plastic bowls typically come in lots of fun colors and shapes, they are lightweight, easy to tip over and move around, and are easily damaged by a chewing Portuguese Water Dog puppy. These bowls can also harbor bacteria in the scratches that are difficult to get clean.

Ceramic bowls can also come in fun colors and designs and are more difficult to knock over and spill. However, these bowls are breakable, so if your Portie does knock one over, it is likely to break or chip. You can mitigate some tipping damage, though, by placing your bowls on a mat.

Stainless steel bowls are both easy to clean and unbreakable, and they are an excellent choice for your Portuguese Water Dog. Some even come with a rubber or silicone base to prevent sliding and spilling.

Another option you will find in a pet store is an elevated bowl set. These are bowls that are set up off the floor so that your dog does not have to bend over as far to eat. These were created to help prevent the serious issue of bloat in some breeds, but studies have shown that elevated feeders can potentially contribute to bloat. Most experts say an elevated feeder is unnecessary and potentially problematic. If you are adopting a dog that has neck or mobility issues, then an elevated dog feeder would be something to discuss with your veterinarian as an option.

Many people also love the convenience of a self-filling water bowl. These bowls have upright jugs of water that funnel into the bowl as the water level is lowered. These can be a great option if you wish to avoid frequently filling the water bowl.

No matter which option you choose, make sure the bowls you purchase are large enough for your Portuguese Water Dog when he is fully grown, or you will likely be buying another set as he grows.

Collar, Tags, and Leash

One of the first things you will want to do when you get your new puppy is to put on his or her collar with identification tags. These tags can be made at any local pet store, or you can order one from an online retailer. It is best to always have your pet's name and your current address and phone number on the tag. This is meant to help a stranger return your dog in the event he ever gets loose. You can even add a little note that says, "Please Call My Family," which may encourage someone to call.

Food

It's important not to abruptly switch your puppy's food when you bring him home, as this can cause digestive upset. Make sure you bring home enough of his current food from the breeder to last a few days, or get the name of the food so you can buy some. If you wish to switch foods, do it gradually over a few days. Regardless, make sure you have your puppy's food planned ahead of time so that you are prepared when he gets hungry!

Toys

Puppies come with lots of energy and razor-sharp teeth. This means if you aren't prepared to give them something to chew on, they will find something around the house to chew on instead. Have a minimum of four or five toys of different varieties to give your puppy so he has plenty of options to keep his attention. You may find that certain types of toys don't last long before being ripped to shreds, or you may find that your Portie loves to care for and carry them with him wherever he goes.

Grooming Brushes

The Portuguese Water Dog requires frequent grooming. Though puppies require less grooming than adults will, it is crucial they become accustomed to the brush early on so that there is no anxiety with it later in life. Begin brushing your Portuguese Water Dog often as a puppy with a small medium-bristle brush. Additional information on grooming will be provided in chapter 12.

Puppy Training Treats

It is helpful to have a safe bag of treats to help with potty training and teaching basic commands in the early days. Look for soft treats that are healthy and natural. Be sure that they contain no animal by-products, are grain-free, and contain absolutely no artificial flavors, colors, or preservatives.

Crate and Pad

The crate is a safe place for your Portuguese Water Dog puppy to be while you are away or when you cannot watch him closely. Though some dislike the idea of crates, they are an important and even imperative part of training when used properly. According to Cheryl Hoofnagle with Blue Run Portuguese Water Dogs, "If you can't have your eye directly on the puppy, it is safer to crate or pen your puppy in a safe area where it can't get into mischief."

Gate or Playpen

Having a safe area to keep your Portie puppy while he plays is extremely helpful. A gate blocking the doorways is an excellent and affordable option. A playpen may be a little pricier, but it is also a great way to keep your puppy safe from harm and your belongings safe from those puppy teeth!

Preparing a Space for Your Portuguese Water Dog

We've already discussed the importance of puppy-proofing your space for your Portuguese Water Dog's safety, but what might that look like practically day-to-day? In this section, we'll go into detail about how to design a puppy-safe play place in a common area of your home so you can keep an eye on your sweet pup without being relegated to puppy duty all day.

Preparing an Indoor Space

> 66
>
> *PWD puppies are mini-sharks—they bite and chew everything in reach. They are more prone to chewing than many breeds. Sit on the floor and look around each room of your house. What you see is what the puppy will try to destroy. Raise plants up, put covers on your electric cords, and find safe places to hide kids' toys and shoes.*
>
> ROBIN L. BURMEISTER
> *Windward Portuguese Water Dogs*
> 99

It is wise to designate a common area of the home, where you spend most of your time, as a puppy play zone and set it up accordingly. This is where the puppy playpen or the door gates will become imperative. At the bare minimum, use a baby gate to block off hallways and other rooms where your Portie may venture out of your sight.

Even better, set up a playpen in the middle of the room, away from furniture and other hazards like electrical cords, and fill it with dog toys

instead. This area needs to be large enough for him to play contentedly for a while but not so large he can still get into puppy mischief.

Remember, this is a temporary arrangement while your dog is young and in training. As your Portuguese Water Dog matures, you will likely be able to expand his freedom little by little until, eventually, he has earned full rein of the house.

Preparing an Outdoor Space

Ample outdoor space is a must for a Portuguese Water Dog. This breed is full of energy and craves a job. If a dog doesn't have an outdoor space to expend some of that energy, he will likely become bored and destructive in the house, by no real fault of his own.

When preparing your outdoor space, it is as important to make it as puppy friendly as your indoor space. Start by removing all chemical products from the area, including the garage. This includes any weed-killers, pesticides, antifreeze, or any other similar products. If you must have them, keep these products out of reach on a very high shelf your Portuguese Water Dog cannot reach. It is

FUN FACT

A Dog By Any Other Name

In Portugal, the PWD has a different name depending on whether it has wavy or curly hair. The wavy-haired dogs are called Cão de Água de Pêlo Ondulados, literally "wavy-haired water dogs." And the curly-haired dogs are called Cão de Água de Pêlo Encaracolados or "curly-haired water dogs."

important to know that these dogs are known as professional "counter surfers" and can likely reach higher spaces than you think.

Fencing is also an important aspect of a dog-safe outdoor space. If you plan to leave your dog outside unsupervised for any length of time, you must have an ample and secure fence. Check existing fencing to make sure there are no gaps, and make sure all gates securely latch. Depending on your individual dog's personality, he may or may not try to go over the fence. If your fence is less than five feet high, this is a possibility you need to be aware of. Also, always double check your dog is wearing his identification tag every time before he is let out, just in case he does find a way out.

A good way to prevent backyard escapes is to stay with your dog. Try not to leave your Portuguese Water Dog outside for extended periods alone. This breed was bred to work alongside humans, and they will not do well alone. A bored Portie is a mischievous one, and sometimes that mischievous nature can cause trouble for both you and him.

Also, just like with indoor plants, some outdoor plants can be toxic as well. Check your outdoor plants and remove the potentially harmful ones before letting your dog explore.

CHAPTER 4

Bringing Home Your Portuguese Water Dog

> "
> *As with any new puppy, the first few days at home should just be about the immediate members of the household bonding with puppy. While everyone is always excited to show off their new puppy, it is important that puppy has identified its new family as a source of safety and comfort in case it becomes overwhelmed with new visitors or situations.*
>
> CHRISTIE KELLO
> *Windward Portuguese Water Dogs*
> "

O nce you have chosen your Portuguese Water Dog and prepared your home, inside and out, you can let the excitement and anticipation build as pick-up day approaches. You may find yourself a bit anxious, wondering how everything will go, but if you follow the tips below, pick-up day should be fun, exciting, and trouble-free.

Picking up Your Portuguese Water Dog

Typically, when you arrive to pick up your puppy from the breeder, he or she will already be separated from the litter awaiting your arrival. Try not to let the excitement of the moment distract you from getting all the information you need from the breeder!

Before leaving with your Portie pup, the breeder should give you detailed information on your puppy's vet records, current shots, future shots, and deworming. They should remind you of any stipulations of the contract or health guarantee and advise you on a feeding schedule. All of this information, as well as breed-specific care tips, should be neatly presented in a packet of some sort, along with registration papers if applicable.

Sometimes a breeder will allow you to take a small blanket or toy home with your dog so that the smell of his litter can comfort him during the transition. Ask ahead of time if this is an option, so you will know if you need to provide the blanket or toy before pick-up day.

> **"**
>
> *Ask your breeder for a comfort toy that smells like the puppy's mom and littermates. This toy will help comfort the puppy at night and throughout the first few days.*
>
> JILL ROUDEBUSH
> *Maritimo Portuguese Water Dogs*
>
> **"**

The Ride Home

Though you may be tempted to travel with your precious new puppy in your lap, it is safest to place your dog in a crate or a puppy harness for the trip. It is not uncommon for a puppy to get motion sickness and vomit on the way home, so you may wish to ask the breeder to withhold food the morning of pick-up day. You may also benefit from bringing a few extra towels just in case a mess needs to be cleaned up along the way.

If you are planning to transport your Portie pup in a crate, know that not all crates will withstand the force of a crash, and some can even become more dangerous for your dog in the event of a crash. When not properly secured to the vehicle, the crate can become a projectile, injuring your puppy and possibly other passengers in the car. You can visit the Center for Pet Safety (CPS) website for a list of tested and approved travel crates.

If you are thinking of buying a harness for your dog to use in the car, know that they are not all created equally. The CPS performed a harness crashworthiness study in 2013, and results showed that only one of the 11 brands tested performed at the level advertised. Some were even deemed "catastrophic failures." Do diligent research on each brand before making your decision, so you can be sure you get a safe harness.

No matter how you travel, always bring water and a bowl for your puppy; even if the drive is short, you never know when an unexpected delay, such as a flat tire, could occur, keeping you out much longer than expected.

Once you are all set up and prepared to leave with your new puppy, allow him to use the restroom on a patch of grass before loading him up. Praise him if he does, and begin your trip home! Try to make the trip home a positive experience for all. If your puppy is anxious, speak calmly to him until you arrive home. Those first few moments together can be a wonderful bonding experience for you both.

> 66
>
> *Young dogs often become car sick. A washable crate pad and a roll of paper towels should be on hand in case puppy gets car sick. Most outgrow this problem in a few months.*
>
> **CHERYL W. HOOFNAGLE**
> *Blue Run Portuguese Water Dogs*
>
> 99

The First Night

> **"**
>
> *Puppies will need to go potty in the middle of the night. Set up a crate next to your bed. When the puppy stirs, quietly take the puppy out of the crate and take it to a designated potty-area. Afterward, quietly put the puppy, with a small treat, back into the crate and go back to bed. Do not turn on all the lights and start talking to your puppy, as it will think it is time to play. I recommend getting up twice during the first few days, and then only once for the next four to six weeks.*
>
> JILL ROUDEBUSH
> *Maritimo Portuguese Water Dogs*
>
> **"**

As previously emphasized, have the house set up before your Portuguese Water Dog makes his arrival. When it is time for the first night, you will need to have a designated place for his crate for bedtime. While some find it easier to get up in the night and let the puppy out if he is in the same room, others feel they cannot sleep while the puppy is whining in their bedroom. If you need to keep your puppy in a separate room, that is fine as long as you can hear him and are able to take him out to potty promptly when he wakes. Try not to move his crate around to different locations, as a predictable routine is most beneficial for both him and you.

Cheryl Hoofnagle with Blue Run Portuguese Water Dogs believes the best place to keep your dog at night is by your bedside. She says, "All puppies suffer separation anxiety when they go to their new homes. Expect a few sleepless nights while you comfort your new puppy in a crate by your bedside."

At bedtime, there are a few things you need to do before crating your puppy for the night. Take your puppy outside and wait for 10 to 15 minutes for him to relieve himself. If the puppy does not, wait 10 minutes, and then try again. Repeat this process for however long it takes your

Photo Courtesy of Bettina Landauer

puppy to go, and then put him directly into the crate for bed with his special blanket or toy from the breeder.

Your puppy will need to go outside to potty at least once during the night. It is best to take him out every time he wakes until potty training is well-established. When you take him out at night, immediately return him to the crate so that he knows nighttime is time for sleep and not play.

The first few nights home can be scary for your puppy, but this is normal. Remember, this phase is temporary, and before you know it, you and your Portuguese Water Dog will be in a routine that will make things easier. If your puppy spends the first night crying in his crate, you may be tempted to take him out and comfort him in your bed. This may seem

*Photo Courtesy of
Steve Makranczy*

like an easy solution, but it is best for everyone, including your puppy, if he learns early on to self-soothe in the crate.

If your puppy is having a difficult time sleeping in the crate or keeps you awake with his crying, try talking to your puppy or rubbing his head through the crate to help calm him. The most important thing you can do in the first few days is to make your puppy feel loved and secure. Bonds you form with each other in the early days will last throughout your dog's lifetime, and they will make all aspects of dog ownership that much more enjoyable. After a few nights, the bedtime whining should stop, and your puppy should come to find his crate a cozy place to sleep.

The First Vet Visit

If your breeder has stipulated that you take your Portuguese Water Dog to the vet within the first few days, you will need to make that appointment ahead of time so that there is no breach of contract. Be sure to take all records from the breeder to that first vet appointment.

The first appointment should just be a general check-up for your puppy to make sure he is in good health. Your Portie will be weighed, and the vet will examine the eyes, ears, nose, heart, and lungs. They will likely look at your puppy's coat condition and examine teeth and mouth. They may take a stool sample to check for parasites and keep the puppy up to date on vaccines if needed.

This appointment should be relatively quick and easy and will likely be filled with lots of exciting "oohs" and "ahhs" over your new Portie pup's fluffy face. Take this opportunity to ask the vet any questions that may have come up about your puppy since you picked him up from the breeder. Don't be afraid to make a list ahead of time so that you don't forget anything.

Cost Breakdown for the First Year

When considering the cost of ownership for a Portuguese Water Dog, it's important to look beyond the purchase price. While the purchase price is often significant upfront, there are several other aspects of ownership that will factor into the overall cost, and you will need to make sure you are financially able to care of all of a Portuguese Water Dog's needs before making the decision to bring one home.

Besides the purchase price or adoption fee of your Portie, consider all the supplies you will need beforehand. Those are mentioned in detail in chapter 3. Food costs for a dog the size of a Portuguese Water Dog can also be significant. Depending on the size of your Portie and the type and brand of food you choose, the cost can be up to $700 a year. Also, keep in mind reoccurring costs, such as toys, chewable bones, beds, replacement collars and leashes, and anything else your dog may need.

Vet bills are another expense and probably the biggest one for dog owners. Depending on where you live, the office fee is about $50, and an exam can be upward of $100. A spay or neuter operation can cost up to $200. Vaccines are relatively cheap at between $20-$30 each, but testing for anything from heartworm to diagnostic bloodwork can cost anywhere from $20-$250. If there is a more serious illness or injury, things can get incredibly expensive in a hurry. X-rays and ultrasounds can cost up to

Photo Courtesy of
Justin J Derevyanik

$300-$400. Anesthesia and surgery procedures for emergencies can run into thousands of dollars.

Pet insurance can help to offset some of these costs, but it can cost an average of $500-$600 per year.

Grooming is another necessary expense. A professional bath is relatively inexpensive, but anything more than that can be quite costly, sometimes running up to $120. This is something your Portuguese Water Dog will need for basic care, so regular grooming needs to be incorporated into the budget.

While many owners train at home, professional training is another cost you may incur. If you opt to seek assistance from a professional, an hour with a private in-home trainer will cost around $100 per session, while a six-week group class costs an average of $200-$300.

If you are a traveler and plan to board your Portuguese Water Dog occasionally, those overnight stays can be pricy, depending on where you live and which facility you choose. Even traveling with your dog can cost extra, so be prepared for those fees as well. Read more about traveling with your dog in chapter 11.

Another cost some will need to take into account is a pet deposit. If you do not own your home, most landlords will require a hefty pet deposit before allowing the dog to reside there. Sometimes these fees can reach into the thousands.

While some of these above costs are optional, many are required to properly care for your Portuguese Water Dog. If you have weighed the cost of ownership for a Portie and believe you can responsibly care for one, this beautiful working breed may be just the one for you!

CHAPTER 5

Being a Puppy Parent

> "
>
> *Short frequent periods of play, exercise, and training are best. Limit training to no more than five minutes at a time. Build experiences with positive reinforcement. Any time your puppy interacts with you, reward the puppy. Break your interactions into small pieces and build on successes. Remember, puppies play hard and then crash. Be careful not to overdo it.*
>
> MARLENE NICEWANDER
> *Cove's End Portuguese Water Dogs*
>
> "

Keeping Expectations Realistic

While Portie puppies are irresistibly cute, taking care of one is a lot of hard work. Along with the adorable puppy moments, there will be difficult and frustrating moments for you as a puppy parent, so it's important to keep your expectations for the first few weeks and months realistic. This chapter will go over all the potential puppy problems you may face and help you navigate them as smoothly as possible. If you are willing to put in the effort now, your Portie pup will reward you with a lifetime of loyalty and love for years to come.

> **"**
>
> *When puppy first goes home, a 'walk' may mean going two houses down the road and back. Once joints are fully formed (around 18 months of age) your puppy can jog and go longer distances with you.*
>
> CHERYL W. HOOFNAGLE
> *Blue Run Portuguese Water Dogs*
>
> **"**

Potential Puppy Problems

Chewing

Chewing can be a big problem for a new puppy parent. Puppies explore the world with their mouths and often use chewing to self-soothe teething pain. Chewing is natural and inevitable, so don't reprimand your puppy for doing it. Instead, try to supply him with ample chew toys or rubber bones that he can safely gnaw. This allows your Portie to chew and protects the legs of your coffee table from harm.

If you catch your puppy chewing on something he shouldn't, remove the item or the puppy from the situation. Give him a stern "no," but don't punish him. Instead, use the positive "take and replace" method by giving him an appropriate chew toy instead. Never let your puppy chew on your fingers, as this can create a bad habit that is difficult to break once established.

Chewing due to teething will likely stop when all the puppy's adult teeth have grown in at around five to six months of age. However, some dogs just like to chew and will continue into adulthood. If your Portie is a consistent chewer, you may want to invest in some bitter-apple spray. Spray this on anything your dog is chewing, and the bad taste should deter him.

> *PWD puppies are very mouthy. Be prepared to work with their biting tendencies by offering alternative options like treats and toys.*
>
> **MARLENE NICEWANDER**
> *Cove's End Portuguese Water Dogs*

Jumping

The Portuguese Water Dog tends to say hello with an enthusiastic jump. While well-intentioned, this excitement can become dangerous to some on the receiving end. Nip this habit in the bud early with training.

When your Portie jumps up, give him a stern "no," then turn and ignore him until he settles. Repeat this over and over. It may take a while, but with persistence, your dog will eventually get the message and learn to keep his paws on the floor.

Resist the urge to give him any attention, even by pushing him off you, as that may become a reaction he seeks.

> *Crate training is essential for PWDs, especially for the first couple of years. They tend to be exuberant and jump a lot when meeting new people. A PWD that is happy and secure in the crate is essential.*
>
> **CHRISTIE KELLO**
> *Windward Portuguese Water Dogs*

Counter Surfing

Portuguese Water Dogs love to counter surf! Their curious nature and hardworking attitude can lead them to mischief, especially when it comes to finding things they want on the counters. Make sure you put away all dangerous items mentioned in Chapter 3, including those tucked back on your countertop. A clever Portie will find a way to reach things.

> **"**
>
> *This breed loves to counter surf. Anything that is left out is considered a snack, so you just need to be prepared for that.*
>
> CHRISTIE KELLO
> *Windward Portuguese Water Dogs*
> **"**

Digging

Dogs dig for many reasons. Some dig out of boredom, some because they are hot and want to lie down in the cool dirt, and some for the sheer joy of it! Not all Portuguese Water Dogs will be diggers, but some may, especially if they aren't being exercised mentally or physically as they should. A bored Portie is much more likely to find himself exhibiting this unwanted behavior.

If your dog does take to the habit of digging, take precautions around your yard to keep both your Portie and your lawn and plants safe. If necessary, you may need to fence off areas you do not want your dog getting his paws into, such as a flower garden.

If your dog is digging under a fence, try to determine why he may be doing it. Is there another animal on the other side demanding his attention? Is he bored and in need of stimulation and adventure? The working nature and adventure-seeking curiosity of the Portuguese Water Dog may lead him to seek a thrill outside of his yard if he isn't getting the stimulation he needs at home.

If you have a dog that just loves to dig holes, try a different approach. Let him outside under supervision only and watch him closely. Once he does his business, offer him a game of fetch or Frisbee to entertain him. If you notice him begin to dig, divert his attention to you and another game.

If you wish to, you may section off a portion of your yard as the "dig zone" and allow your dog to dig there safely. By allowing him a corner to dig, you may save yourself some flowerbed heartache. While it may not be ideal for you, it is a compromise to allow the dog to do what he loves in a less destructive manner.

Barking and Growling

Barking and growling are normal for a Portuguese Water Dog puppy. If you're in the middle of a tug-of-war match with your new pup, and he lets out a vicious growl, worry not. It doesn't mean he is showing aggression. This is just the nature of puppy play and is exactly how he would be playing with his littermates.

If you want to discourage play fighting, don't do it by punishing your puppy. These are natural behaviors that should simply be ignored. Even an older Portie may bark and growl with you while playing. If your puppy or grown dog begins to play too rough and bark and growl, stop playing immediately and walk away. Come back when the dog settles down. If your dog continues to play too rough, repeat the process until your dog grasps the idea of what is and is not acceptable. This will take time but is well worth the effort.

If your Portie seems truly agitated or begins nipping and biting in a way that seems defensive, it may be time to schedule a trip to see the vet. Truly agitated growling and biting behavior in a previously well-mannered dog can indicate a health problem that may be causing your dog pain.

Separation Anxiety

A Portuguese Water Dog will not do well alone for any extended period of time. This breed was bred to work alongside human companions, and that is what the dogs desire to do, still to this day. A bored and lonely Portie can become anxious and destructive. While it is normal for many dogs to whine or bark when left alone for a short time, this behavior typically stops as they become accustomed to short spans alone. However, a dog with true separation anxiety will bark and pace persistently until you return.

Some signs of separation anxiety in your Portie may be destructive behaviors like chewing and clawing things while you're gone and even defecating in the house. Even a house-trained dog may urinate or defecate in the house repeatedly when left alone if he suffers from separation anxiety. In extreme cases, a dog may display signs of coprophagia, a condition when a dog defecates and then consumes his stool.

It may be helpful to take your dog for a walk or play fetch with him for a while just before you leave the house. Hopefully, this will tire your dog out, and he will be too exhausted to get worked up while you're gone. You can also try leaving your dog with an interactive toy. Try a treat ball or a dog puzzle that will reward him with treats periodically. This may be just enough distraction to get your dog through his time alone. Make this toy or puzzle a special thing your dog only gets when he's alone. This can help positively reinforce that being alone can be a treat.

If the separation anxiety is severe and nothing seems to work, make an appointment with your vet to check that there is nothing else going on. They may be able to advise you on some safe ways to keep your dog calm when you have to leave the house for short periods of time.

> **"**
>
> *PWDs will pitch a fit in their crate. Ignore them. Never take a puppy who is throwing a tantrum out of the crate. The breed is very smart and doing so once will generally buy you about four extra nights of sleep deprivation. And always pick up a pack of soft earplugs for your family before your puppy arrives. I've been thanked countless times for this tip!*
>
> **ROBIN L. BURMEISTER**
> *Windward Portuguese Water Dogs*
> **"**

Crate Training

Dogs are not true den animals by nature, but they do need a safe and quiet place to retreat to when they feel scared or anxious. In the wild, dogs and wolves only den when they rear puppies. These dens are usually holes dug in the ground by the mother wolf. The holes are abandoned when the puppies are old enough to travel with the pack. Although domesticated dogs' ancestors didn't spend their days in a den, that doesn't mean your new puppy won't find comfort in a "den" of his own in your house.

Crate training can be controversial among animal lovers. Some believe it to be inhumane and too cage-like. Others believe a crate is a necessary training tool used to protect and secure a dog. The fact is, using a crate for training makes puppy ownership more convenient for you and safer for your pup. When done properly, crating your dog is an excellent tool for house-training and will set your dog up for success from the beginning.

There are multiple crate options to choose from. Some are plastic, some are wire, some are soft shell, and some are heavy-duty. The two main crate types are plastic and wire. If you're planning to travel with your Portie, you will need a plastic crate, as this is the only type the airlines allow.

Another common crate type is the wire crate. These allow more visibility and airflow for your Portie. These crates are typically collapsible and are easily stored when not in use. Depending on the size, some wire crates come with a divider to section off the crate. This is a nice feature that allows for a smaller puppy to grow into a larger crate so that you don't have to purchase multiple crates as he grows.

HELPFUL TIP

An Allergy-Friendly Option

Like poodles, Portuguese Water Dogs have a single, low-shedding coat that more closely resembles hair than fur. This curly or wavy coat is ideal for people who suffer from mild-to-moderate allergies to pet dander. While PWDs have no undercoat and don't shed as much as other breeds, they do lose some hair and require frequent brushing and grooming to prevent painful matting.

Photo Courtesy of
Valerie Hawk

Whichever type you choose, line your crate with a commercial crate pad or with a towel or blanket for comfort. You want the crate to be inviting and become a comfortable spot for your Portie to retreat.

The key to successful crate training is positive reinforcement. Do not ever put your dog in the crate as a form of punishment. This sends the message that the crate is a bad place and will create issues going forward. You don't want your dog to view the crate as a "timeout" box, or he will never retreat there willingly.

The first time you introduce your new puppy to the crate, you'll want to have some training treats on hand. Secure the door of the crate to the side so that it doesn't accidentally swing closed and scare your puppy. Begin by placing a treat or two outside, near the door of the crate. Depending on how your dog reacts to the crate, slowly place the treats closer until you can put one inside. Your puppy should voluntarily go inside the crate to get the treat.

Don't shut the door of the crate the first few times the puppy goes in. Instead, praise him and allow him to come in and out of the crate freely.

Photo Courtesy of Nicole Sendar

After your puppy becomes comfortable with the open crate, guide him inside and gently latch the door. Give him treats from outside the crate and verbally praise him. Only leave him in there for a few moments at first and stay with him. This will help him feel comfortable. Practice this exercise the first day you get your puppy home to get him comfortable with the crate before his first night in it.

Any time you need to crate your dog, do so by rewarding him with treats and a special toy. Praise him and make it a fun experience to get inside the crate. Don't leave your dog in the crate for long the first few times, except for nighttime, or he may begin to get anxious and associate those feelings with the crate. Practice leaving your puppy in the crate while you're home for short increments of time, 30 minutes to an hour. Always immediately take your dog outside to his potty area when you let him out of the crate.

Be sure to exercise your dog thoroughly before expecting him to have any crate time. It is not reasonable for you to put your dog in a crate without first allowing him to expend his energy. Doing this will allow him to rest and sleep in his crate while you're away, further minimizing the chances of separation anxiety.

A crate is a tool that needs to be used responsibly. Never leave your Portie in the crate for an extended period. Also, never treat the crate like a dog-sitter. With proper training, your puppy will outgrow his need for the crate and will no longer need to be confined to it while you're sleeping or away. If your puppy doesn't view the crate as a place of rest and comfort, you may need to reevaluate the way you're using it.

> **❝**
>
> *I think it is very important that a dog is crate trained. It really gives the dog its own place to go if need be, and it works well if you need to make sure your dog is not able to run out the door or get underfoot.*
>
> PATTI MCKNIGHT
> *McKnight's PWDs*
>
> **❞**

Leaving Your Portuguese Water Dog Home Alone

> **"**
>
> *I warn people that a bored PWD is a naughty PWD. They will find interesting and creative ways to entertain themselves, so you have to always keep a sense of humor.*
>
> CHRISTIE KELLO
> *Windward Portuguese Water Dogs*
>
> **"**

The first time you leave your Portuguese Water Dog at home alone can be a nerve-wracking experience for you both. Hopefully, you have already taken the time to acquaint your dog with the crate and made it a positive space for him. Before leaving him for the first time, plan to play with him vigorously or take him on a long walk. This can help wear him out before you go in hopes that he may simply lie down and nap while you're away.

Photo Courtesy of
Steve Makranczy

When it is time for you to leave, follow the same guidelines previously mentioned. Reward your dog with a treat for entering the crate and give him a special "crate only" toy as an additional reward and boredom buster. Interactive treat toys like Kong work great for this.

Photo Courtesy of Chris and Jon Zombek

When you return from your first trip away, it may seem fitting to greet your puppy with an excited hello, but refrain so that you don't make your dog think getting out of the crate is more exciting than going in. Going in the crate should be fun and exciting, and getting out should be no big deal. Open the door with little fuss and promptly take your dog outside to do his business. This will help to keep your dog from becoming overexcited every time you let him out of the crate.

Crate training is a process, and it takes both time and effort. Some dogs take to the crate easily, and some take a little more time and practice. Your Portie will not like to be left alone, as they are high-energy companion dogs. This means it is highly important that you do not overuse the crate and make the dog associate it with the negative feelings of being left alone. If you do need to regularly leave your dog home alone, reconsider getting a Portuguese Water Dog, as that is not a life he will enjoy.

CHAPTER 6

Potty Training Your Portuguese Water Dog

Potty Training Methods

There are two basic training methods employed by trainers—positive reinforcement and negative reinforcement. More information about each of these methods can be found in chapter 10, but it is important to know that the best way to potty train your Portuguese Water Dog is through positive reinforcement. You may have heard to "rub your dog's nose in it" when he's had an accident, but we now know that not only is that method not effective, it is a cruel punishment for a puppy who doesn't know better.

The goal of potty training is to teach your Portie that your home is also his home. Instinctually, dogs will not soil the places where they eat and sleep. Until your dog is potty trained, you will need to keep him confined to a small, controlled area of your home so he does not go off into an unused corner to relieve himself. This area could be a puppy playpen in the same room as you when you first begin potty training. As the potty training progresses, you will be able to expand the areas your dog can go until, eventually, he may have the run of the house, if that is what you desire.

Photo Courtesy of
Valerie Hawk

Take your puppy out often, about every hour, and reward him freely with verbal praise and treats. Try to consistently take him to the same area so he will smell his scent and know that it's time to potty. Make this time with your puppy calm and all about the business. Do your best to ignore his attempts to play until after he's finished so that he doesn't forget the reason he went outside in the first place.

It may take 10 to 15 minutes, but when your dog relieves himself, celebrate enthusiastically and reward him with a training treat. This will help show him that going potty outside is a positive and fun experience. Your Portie is bright and wants to learn, so when he begins to understand that relieving himself outside is what you want, potty training should go much easier.

> *Manage the process. Take them to the same place every time so they begin to understand where you want that behavior. Verbally reward them when they go potty where and when you want them to.*
>
> MARLENE NICEWANDER
> *Cove's End Portuguese Water Dogs*

Using the Crate for Potty Training

The crate is a great tool to use for potty training because it allows you to control your puppy in a small space during the times you can't supervise him. If you're using a wire crate, install the divider inside so that the area is big enough for your dog to comfortably stand and turn around but not big enough that he can take several steps to the other side. This will prevent him from soiling one side and sleeping on the other.

Jill Roudebush from Maritimo Portuguese Water Dogs in Ohio says,

> *"A crate is the single most important tool when house breaking a puppy. The crate area should only be large enough for the puppy to comfortably turn around. Most crates come with dividers that can be adjusted as the puppy grows. If you are unable to watch your puppy, let the puppy potty and put it in its crate. When your puppy is out and playing, take it out every 45 minutes no matter what. Puppies' bladders are immature, and they are not able to hold it for very long. Puppies will need to potty immediately upon waking, after playing, and after eating. This is true even if they were just out."*

If you're unsure how often you should take your new Portuguese Water Dog outside, a good rule of thumb to follow for a young puppy is for every month old he is, that's how many hours he can wait to go potty.

That doesn't mean that you should only take your puppy out that often because if you do, you will most likely be cleaning up a lot of accidents. This is simply a guideline for how long a young puppy can be left in the crate before he must go out. Never leave your puppy or dog in the crate longer than four to six hours, except at night.

When you wake up in the morning, immediately take your dog outside to the designated potty area. If you're planning to put your dog back into the crate while you're gone for work, take the time to exercise him thoroughly before you do. This will help your dog rest better while you're gone. You will need to come home to let your dog out at lunchtime. Follow the same procedure before putting him back into the crate. However, this is not an ideal life for a Portie. If you plan to leave your dog home in the crate while you are away at work often, you should reconsider ownership, as this breed will not enjoy being left alone daily.

If you must leave your dog for a time daily, consider puppy daycare instead. Not only will this allow you to socialize your dog, but it will also be a fun place for him to play and use his energy up while you are away. Usually, these places require certain vaccinations, so be sure to call and check ahead of time. If doggy daycare is not an option, call a friend or family member to come by and let your puppy out for you. You can even hire a dog walker to come and exercise your pup while you are away. Go through a reputable service like Care.com so you can read references and know they've had a background check.

If you absolutely must leave your dog in the crate or a puppy-proofed room for longer than you should, you can use a puppy pad on one side of the crate. This will slow down the training process because you will, at some point, have to remove the pads and retrain your dog that the only acceptable place to go is outside. Again, if you will be consistently leaving your dog in the crate for extended periods of time, you may need to consider the well-being of your dog and explore other options. Portuguese Water Dogs love their people and will not be happy spending most of the day alone.

The First Few Weeks

> **"**
>
> *Potty training goes more smoothly if the pup is confined to its crate at night and is taken out the same door and to the same area of the yard to do its business. 'Potty outside' is the phrase we teach pups from four weeks old, so they are mostly potty trained before they go home. We instruct owners to take the pup outside upon waking and after meals at a minimum, and to watch for when the pup goes to the door.*
>
> CATHERINE M. DUGAN
> *Aviator Kennels*
>
> **"**

Don't let anyone tell you potty training a puppy is easy. Potty training takes time and patience and probably a few bottles of carpet cleaner. Despite the challenges the first few weeks present, know that there is light at the end of the tunnel. Through the frustrations and accidents, your Portie will eventually figure it out, and your life together will become much less stressful.

Potty training begins the day you bring your Portie pup home. In the beginning, take your dog out every 45 minutes to an hour during daytime hours. He may not need to go every time, but give him 10 to 15 minutes to try. Even if you have a fenced backyard, it will benefit you to take your dog outside on a leash. This will allow you to control where he goes and help him not to be too distracted.

Rewarding Good Behavior

Positive reinforcement is essentially rewarding your dog for good behavior, such as going potty outside and not inside. So, don't forget to praise him verbally and with a treat as soon as he finishes. Remember, your Portie wants to please you, so if you can effectively communicate what you want from him and learn to read his signals, potty training can become a breeze!

> *They learn very quickly. Use the same in and out door for consistency. Go out and say 'potty' and then offer tons of praise when the puppy goes!*
>
> ROBIN L. BURMEISTER
> *Windward Portuguese Water Dogs*

How to Handle Accidents

> *Carry a young pup outside so it doesn't stop and pee along the way to the door.*
>
> ROBIN L. BURMEISTER
> *Windward Portuguese Water Dogs*

Accidents are going to happen, so go ahead and buy that odor-neutralizing cleaner! Learning to potty outside is tough for a young puppy and requires patience by all. If you have been trying to train your dog to go on the grass, accidents on rugs and carpets are inevitable. The feeling of the carpet on a dog's paws is very similar to the feeling of grass and can sometimes trick a young puppy into thinking he can relieve himself there. If this becomes a problem, you might want to temporarily remove any rugs from your puppy's designated area until he gets the hang of going outside.

If you catch your Portie in the moment of an accident, quickly pick him up and take him outside to the potty area. Don't punish or yell at your dog; simply give a stern "no" and take him outside. Accidents are inevitable and are often the result of the owner not taking the puppy out as often as he needs. Still, sometimes a dog will soil the carpet a mere minute after coming inside. Regardless, your Portie pup is still learning and should not be punished for the mistake. Punishing only causes confusion and prolongs the potty training process.

Doggy Door Pros and Cons

Doggy doors can be beneficial in your effort to potty train, especially for older dogs. If you have a secure backyard, a doggy door can allow your dog to let himself out as he pleases. This could mean fewer accidents and a shorter training period. You should never let your dog go outside unsupervised unless you know the backyard is completely secure and your dog can't escape. Adding a doggy door is not for everyone, though, and you should review this list of pros and cons before making your decision.

Installation

Installing a doggy door is making a permanent change to your home, and they are notoriously difficult to install. If you don't own your home, a doggy door is probably not an option for you.

Unwanted Visitors

Doggy doors are great for allowing your dog to freely come in and out of your home, but they may unintentionally offer that same freedom to unwanted wild animals as well. A Portuguese Water Dog will need a large doggy door, which means it could become an entry point for a thief or even a much smaller masked bandit, like a raccoon! Buy one with a locking function to avoid this issue at night.

FUN FACT

Fast Learners

Portuguese Water Dogs are brilliant and eager to please. Their biddable disposition and higher-than-average intelligence make them remarkably easy to train, which is excellent news for the potty-training PWD owner. With consistency and positive reinforcement, most PWDs learn the ins and outs of potty training between eight and 12 weeks old.

Photo Courtesy of
Ana Donlan

Indoor Cats

If you have an indoor cat, it will be nearly impossible to keep him from leaving through the doggy door. If your cat has been declawed, this is particularly dangerous because your cat will have no defense from predators. If you have an indoor cat who already loves to go outside, a doggy door will allow him to bring his "treasures" inside the house. Finding a dead snake or bird in the house is probably not what the doggy door was meant for.

Securing the Yard

Before allowing your dog unsupervised time in the yard, you must be sure it's a safe area. Be sure the fence is secure, and add a lock to any gate so neighborhood kids or thieves cannot let your dog out. If your dog is a digger, then you may have a problem with him digging out to go explore.

Photo Courtesy of Jon Zombek

Backyard Pool

Another danger to consider in the backyard is a pool. Even though your Portuguese Water Dog is likely a fantastic swimmer, he should never be allowed near the pool unless you are out there with him, just in case of an accident. Swimming alone is dangerous, even for a dog like the Portie. Allowing full access to the house and pool also permits your dog to come in and out freely while sopping wet, causing a big mess for you to clean up when you get home.

Fire Escape

One positive to a doggy door is it allows your dog to escape the house in case of an emergency. This could potentially save your dog's life in the event of a fire.

If you know your yard is safe and secure, and you want to install a doggy door to aid in training, go ahead! You will still need to confine your dog's indoor privileges to a small space while still allowing access to the doggy door. This can be done by using a playpen set up against the wall.

A doggy door is not always a good option, but in the right scenario, it can be very helpful. For elderly or disabled owners who have a more difficult time getting around, a doggy door allows the dog to relieve himself in the proper area without any burden on the owner.

If you decide on a doggy door, be prepared for a little bit of training; your puppy will not know how to use it otherwise. The first time you teach him to use it, give him a gentle push through and have another person on the other side ready with a small treat and plenty of praise. Do this several times in both directions. Once your puppy allows you to push him through without resistance, go to the opposite side of the doggy door, extend your hand through to the puppy, and allow him to smell the treat in your hand. Use the treat to lure him through. Finally, call him from the other side, and give him a treat when he goes through by himself. If you spend five or 10 minutes a day doing this, your Portuguese Water Dog should be going through the door by himself within a week.

CHAPTER 7

Socializing Your Portuguese Water Dog

> *They are happiest when they are with their owners and when they have a job to do. If you don't want a dog who is constantly by your side, then this is not the breed for you.*
>
> CHERYL W. HOOFNAGLE
> *Blue Run Portuguese Water Dogs*

Importance of Socialization

Portuguese Water Dogs love their people fiercely and typically also do well with other people and even other dogs if they have been properly socialized. By beginning your dog's socialization early, you can be sure that he will be able to coexist with any people or dogs he encounters in any environment. This will make life easier for you and for him as he will inevitably encounter other humans and animals regularly throughout his life, whether it be on a hike, a stroll through town, or even at a restaurant.

Behavior around Other Dogs

Dogs have their own code of social etiquette, which is much different from ours. Imagine if we greeted each other the way dogs do by sniffing, circling, and jumping up and down playfully. That would be a silly sight! Luckily, our social rules are a bit stricter than theirs. However, dogs understand these behaviors a little differently than we do, and oftentimes dog-to-dog behaviors that we may find strange are completely normal.

Much like people, dogs greet each other differently at a first meeting than they greet an old friend. Oftentimes these encounters depend on the individual dog's personality as well. Dogs typically greet each other in one or all of the following ways:

Sniffing

Probably the most notable canine ritual is the sniff test. When dogs greet one another, they may begin with the muzzle or go straight for the backside. Sometimes the sniff will be brief, and sometimes it can seem like a full-blown investigation. Unless one dog seems uncomfortable, this is perfectly normal behavior and doesn't need to be stopped. Once the dogs have satisfied their sniffers, they can move on to the next step in the canine greeting.

Play Stance

Have you ever seen a dog approach another dog and immediately go into a play bow? This behavior is simply one dog attempting to initiate play with another. It's like he's saying, "Hey there! Do you want to be friends and play together?" Even a quick, playful growl accompanied by a friendly tail wag is acceptable. Again, as long as neither dog seems stressed, there is no need to stop this behavior. Even if the other dog declines the offer to play, that doesn't mean the meeting was not successful.

Exerting Dominance

This greeting is probably the least endearing, but it is still acceptable in the canine world. One dog may exert his dominance by being the first to sniff and by non-aggressively showing the other dog he is in charge. This could include mounting. This process may be obvious to you, or it may all happen so quickly that you don't even notice until one dog rolls over to show his belly in submission. As with the other behaviors, these are the natural social ways of dogs and should not be stopped unless there is real aggression or stress. Dogs take social cues well and are pretty good at keeping each other in line. If one dog is not satisfied with another's behavior, he will probably let the other know.

Knowing these common dog behaviors and greetings can help you determine how things are going when your Portie is socializing with other dogs. Learning to read your dog's behavior can help prepare you to know when you may need to step in and separate the dogs. Safety is always the key when socializing your Portuguese Water Dog.

> **"**
>
> *Find other puppies about the same age and size. Arrange play-dates with other neutral dogs. Don't force situations that make your puppy uncomfortable. Watch your puppy's reaction and, if you observe a lack of confidence, keep your puppy under the threshold of discomfort. You are responsible for making sure your puppy feels safe at all times.*
>
> MARLENE NICEWANDER
> *Cove's End Portuguese Water Dogs*
>
> **"**

Safe Ways to Socialize

> **"**
>
> *Meeting older dogs is not a priority. Playdates with littermates or selected adult dogs that are both healthy and gentle with puppies is fine, but avoid dog parks where an aggressive dog can terrify your puppy and leave him permanently scarred by the experience.*
>
> CHERYL W. HOOFNAGLE
> *Blue Run Portuguese Water Dogs*
>
> **"**

When socialization begins early, you are setting your Portie up for a life of adaptability. Because puppies are, in general, playful and eager to meet other playmates, getting him accustomed to other dogs should be relatively easy early on. Socialization should begin as early as possible, but be sure not to allow your puppy to have close contact with dogs you don't know until he has had his complete series of puppy shots.

Patti McKnight with McKnights PWDs in Illinois says,

> **66**
>
> *I think one of the best activities to help socialize Portuguese Water Dogs is to have them enrolled in a puppy class. The class will have age-appropriate puppies, and most are curious about other pups. You should never put your Portuguese Water Dog unsupervised with any other dog. Dogs can react in a negative way super-fast.*
>
> **99**

When socializing with other dogs outside of a controlled environment like a puppy class, there are differing opinions on how this should be done. Some professionals believe all first greetings should be done

with restraints or barriers, just in case. Others believe these barriers and restraints cause stress for all dogs involved and can elevate the tension. They believe that dogs that are allowed to freely greet each other can do so more comfortably without feeling trapped.

If you choose to socialize your puppy with a leash on, keep your puppy close on a leash or on the other side of a barrier, such as a gate, when you make introductions with other dogs, especially those that are older or larger. Preferably all other dogs should also be leashed or some-how restrained in case anything goes wrong.

Allow the dogs to greet each other for a few seconds and then walk away. Each owner should distract their dog at this point until they are no longer interested in the other dog. If the initial interaction went well, allow the dogs to come together again in the same manner. Keep the leash loose so the dog can maneuver but not so loose it becomes a tan-gled mess. Read each dog's body language to determine how the greeting is going. Bodies should be relaxed, and there should be no staring con-tests. As the dogs become comfortable and relaxed with each other, you will be able to let them off-leash, and they can have supervised play.

If you choose the no-leash method, make sure all first greetings are done in a neutral location so that no dog can feel territorial and defensive. Allow the dogs to meet, but monitor their body language. If they use the body language described above, you don't need to interfere. But if either dog seems stiff, uncom-fortable, or agitated, separate the dogs and use distractions to get their attention off each other. Off-leash greetings can bring a greater risk if you don't know the other dog well and should only be done with friendly, pre-socialized dogs.

FUN FACT

A Kennedy Favorite

Senator Ted Kennedy was a huge proponent of Portuguese Water Dogs and enjoyed many PWD companions. Portuguese Water Dogs Sunny, Cappy, and Splash were permanent fixtures at the late senator's side. Kennedy's beloved Sunny gained literary immor-tality when the senator penned the children's book My Senator and Me: *A Dog's Eye View of Washington, DC,* in 2006. The last of Senator Kennedy's PWDs, Splash, passed away in 2010 at the age of 13.

Safety is the most important thing when socializing your dog, so only do what you feel comfortable with.

Socializing an adult Portuguese Water Dog can be a bit more challenging if he has not been properly socialized from puppyhood. If you are adopting an adult Portuguese Water Dog, he may have experienced some trauma in his life that causes challenges when socializing with other dogs. Often with a rescue, you don't know exactly what his life has held up until the point he was rescued. He may have been kept in a cage his whole life, abused by his owner, or even been previously attacked by a dog. All these things are unknowns that could have a significant impact on the dog's social abilities.

If this is the case, time and patience are needed by both you and your dog. Allow your Portie to socialize on his own terms, even if it is in small increments. Avoid putting your dog in situations that cause him more stress, as this will not help him but rather hinder his progress.

Begin socializing your adult Portie at home. Take your dog on a walk through the neighborhood so he can see other dogs but not necessarily

Photo Courtesy of Cindy McCue

interact with them yet. With much time and persistence, he should eventually become comfortable enough to walk by other dogs in their backyards or on leashes without becoming stressed. When he has successfully mastered these indirect encounters, it's time to move on to the next step.

If you have a neighbor with a dog, this is a great place to start direct socialization if they are willing. These dogs will probably encounter each other at one point or another and will benefit from getting to know each other. Ask your neighbor and arrange a time to allow both dogs to meet in a neutral part of the yard. Take things slow and give them space if either dog seems stressed. Follow the three-second rule and then walk away and distract each dog. Allow the dogs to come together again if the first encounter went well. If it doesn't seem to be going well, that's okay! Allow the dogs to just be in the yard at the same time until they become used to each other, and then gradually allow them to interact more as it seems appropriate.

If you don't have a neighboring dog, call a friend or family member with a dog. If the dogs get along well, try to set up regular playdates with dog friends so that your pup can continue to work on socialization skills. Weekly walks at the park together or even off-leash playtime at each other's homes may be possible once the dogs get to know each other.

A dog park is another option to meet other dogs, but not a good one. These parks can be overwhelming, depending on how many dogs are there. This option is a last resort as a place to socialize.

If you must visit a dog park, begin by just walking around the perimeter at a comfortable distance. Listen to your dog and take his cues. If he seems comfortable, allow him to interact more closely with a dog through the fence. If he remains calm, praise him. Reward him for positive encounters and remove him from negative ones. Try to only let him interact with dogs that are also calm. It will not help the situation to engage with a loud, barking, rambunctious dog through the fence. This could cause stress for an unsocialized dog and stop progress.

More important than progress is comfort and security for your dog. He needs to feel safe with you above all, and if that means socialization progresses slowly, it is better to take baby steps with a challenging Portie than to cause him undue stress by trying to force him into social situations he isn't ready for.

Greeting New People

Puppies generally meet new people with ease, especially a well-bred Portuguese Water Dog. The biggest challenge you will face when introducing your puppy to new humans is likely going to be his jumping habit. This can be challenging because when your puppy is small, the jumping may seem cute. However, once the dog grows into a medium to large adult dog, the jumping becomes a problem, and it's much harder to correct the behavior if it was once allowed.

Ideally, when approached by a person, your puppy should remain calm and keep all four paws on the ground. If you need to stop a jumping habit, begin by teaching your dog an alternate command. "Sit" is a good command to combat jumping because your dog can't do both at the same time. When your dog gets overly excited and begins to jump, counter by giving the "sit" command. Reward him for sitting and staying calm. If he can't stay calm and continues to jump, leave the room as suggested in Chapter 5 and ignore your dog for 30 seconds to one minute. Return and try again. This process works well for meeting new

people, getting the leash out for walks, or any other exciting event that gets your dog jumping.

Helping a rescued Portie meet new people may not go as smoothly, depending on his past interactions with humans. If your Portie has social challenges and seems nervous around humans, begin new introductions slowly so as not to stress him too much. You and anyone you introduce him to will need to work to earn his trust, and depending on his past, that may take much time and patience.

If you're having guests over, ask those people ahead of time to remain calm and not show the dog much attention. This may help ease your dog's mind and keep him calm. If your guests want to rub and love all over your pup, even with the best intentions, it could cause him to become overexcited and stressed. Once calm and comfortable, the dog may be trusting enough to allow a belly rub or two, but it should always be on his own terms. Give your guests some training treats to gain his trust. If your dog is particularly shy and nervous, and you don't see much progress being made, try separating him with a baby gate so that he can observe the people but not feel pressured or overwhelmed.

Other ways you can socialize your Portie are taking him out to dog-friendly stores and meeting people. Big-box hardware stores are a great place for this. They are typically dog-friendly and full of people who will find it hard to resist the urge to ask you about your Portie! Have a few small treats handy and ask people to give one to your dog—he will quickly learn that meeting people is a good experience.

Portuguese Water Dogs and Children

> 66
>
> *PWDs thrive when given a job, including watching over children or hiking with the family.*
>
> CATHERINE M. DUGAN
> *Aviator Kennels*
> 99

If introduced to children at an early age, your Portuguese Water Dog will likely do wonderfully with them. He will become loyal to them just as he is to you. Allowing your children to participate in your Portie's training sessions can further strengthen the bond they will have. Give them some training treats and show them how to teach the "sit" command, as described in Chapter 10. Not only will your puppy learn to respect your children, but your children will learn patience and other valuable life lessons!

Porties are generally good with young kids; however, for everyone's safety, it is important to always closely supervise any dog-to-child socialization. This is simply good dog parenting. A loving Portuguese Water Dog shouldn't show aggression toward kids but is more likely to accidentally cause injury with a friendly jump. This is another reason to nip that habit in the bud as early as possible.

Always teach your children to be gentle and kind, never pulling ears, hair, or tail. Show them by example the proper way to pet your Portuguese Water Dog so that they understand how to safely handle him. No matter how friendly and trustworthy your dog is, never leave a child and dog alone unattended. This is for the safety of both the child and the dog.

CHAPTER 8

Portuguese Water Dogs and Your Other Pets

Introducing Your New Puppy to Existing Pets

> **"**
>
> *Many people who get a PWD want a second one. Like potato chips, you can't just have one! If you are considering a second dog, it's best to introduce the puppy before the older dog is seven years old. An opposite-sex puppy to your current dog is the safest choice, as same-sex dogs don't always get along.*
>
> CHERYL W. HOOFNAGLE
> *Blue Run Portuguese Water Dogs*
>
> **"**

When bringing home a new Portuguese Water Dog, you may be wondering how to introduce him to any other existing pets you have at home. Whether it's a cat or another small animal, there are certain precautions you should take to help introductions go well and encourage positive relationships to build.

It is crucial that you begin interspecies relationships as early as possible. A Portuguese Water Dog can do well with a cat if he is introduced to one as a puppy. When introducing your new Portie puppy to a resident cat, take caution to do it with care so that they can get off on the right foot.

Begin by keeping your puppy and cat separated. Place a blanket or toy with the puppy's scent near the cat. Do the same for the puppy in a different area of the house. Let the dog and the cat sniff and become accustomed to the scents before a face-to-face interaction.

After exchanging scents, allow your pets to interact indirectly. Keep them separated by a gate or the crate, but allow them to view each other. Depending on their reactions, you may feel comfortable enough to let them loose, but be careful—your puppy probably can't do much damage to your cat (depending on his age and size), but your cat can definitely harm your puppy if he feels threatened.

Try introductions with someone gently holding each animal. Let the two sniff and explore, but watch carefully for claws. Praise both animals for calm and reasonable reactions. Stop the introduction immediately if there is any fear or aggression shown.

Most likely, your Portie pup will want to make friends with your cat and play right away. Your cat, on the other hand, probably won't know how to handle all of this playful energy and curiosity and will need a place to escape. This escape should be off the ground in an area where your dog can't reach. Allow your cat to leave the situation whenever he needs to.

Introducing an Older Portuguese Water Dog

Introducing an older Portuguese Water dog to a cat can be more difficult and harder to predict. Before adopting an adult Portie with an existing cat at home, make sure he does well with cats in general. If you know your Portie has issues with cats, your home may not be the right fit for him. There is no need to stress an adult dog by introducing him to a home with other animals if he prefers to be an only pet.

Introductions need to be done carefully, as an adult dog can cause real harm to a cat and vice versa. Begin with the same scent exchange described above. After a day of letting the animals get accustomed to each other's scent, allow the two to meet through a closed door. Depending on individual personality, either pet may not be very interested in the other, or the animals may be busting down the door to see who is on the other side. Allow each animal to become calm and relaxed before any face-to-face interactions.

Once the two have become relaxed and calm on both sides of the door, allow the animals to meet with the dog on a loose leash. Allow a brief interaction before separating them and diverting their attention. If the initial interaction was calm and peaceful, try again. If you decide to let the two interact with your dog off-leash, always ensure your cat can escape to his safe space, designated just for him.

Cats and dogs can live peacefully together and can even form close bonds, but it may not happen overnight, and that is okay. Just because it takes time doesn't mean your pets won't eventually have a tight-knit relationship.

Fighting/Bad Behavior

Portuguese Water Dogs are not known for aggressive behavior; however, despite proper breeding and good genetics, improper treatment can cause certain aggression issues in any dog. These behaviors are especially important to understand if you're bringing home a rescue Portie with an unknown past. Understanding possible triggers and reactions can help you better understand your Portie and help him overcome these unfair obstacles he faces.

HELPFUL TIP

Family Dog?
Yay or Nay?

Portuguese Water Dogs are extremely intelligent and athletic. These dogs typically do well with children, especially older children who can handle this dog's energetic disposition. PWDs need plenty of exercise and enjoy going out to meet new friends. In addition, their low prey drive makes them excellent additions to homes with other small dogs or cats.

If your dog displays any aggressive behaviors, such as growling or snapping, the first thing you should do is take him to the vet to rule out any underlying conditions. Sometimes, unbeknownst to the owner, a dog can actually be in pain, which causes him to become irritable and react aggressively to certain situations. Treating the underlying pain can help your Portie stop the aggression altogether.

Once this is ruled out as a cause, evaluate your dog's current situation. Is there something causing him stress? A life change? Is he being left alone too long? Are you meeting his energy requirements and his need for adventure? Remember, a Portuguese Water Dog is a very high-energy companion dog, and they desire to work alongside you day in and day out. Any degree of neglect can cause behavioral issues that are not the dog's fault.

If your Portie is showing aggression toward other dogs, it may be a lack of proper socialization. Go back to Chapter 7 and learn how to socialize your dog safely. Dogs dealing with aggression issues may progress slowly, so take your time and don't rush him into a situation that could cause setbacks or even injure him or another dog.

If your dog is showing aggression toward other pets at home, begin by identifying the source. Food aggression is a common issue among pets at home. Does your dog become possessive of toys or treats? If you identify the source of aggression, remove it.

If your dog is dealing with food aggression, eliminate the situation by feeding your Portie in another room, away from all other pets. If he is particularly possessive of a favorite toy, only allow him to have the toy within the confines of his crate or designated alone area. Removing your dog from the stressful situation will not solve the aggression problem, but it will make life easier while you deal with the root cause.

If your dog isn't causing any physical harm to you or any other members of your family, continue to work on carefully socializing the dog and rewarding friendly behavior with treats and praise. If the aggression doesn't improve or evolves to physical harm in any way, seek a professional trainer's help immediately. Never leave a potentially aggressive dog alone or unrestrained with another animal or an unfamiliar person.

When Is the Aggression too Much?

Dogs frequently growl and bare their teeth when they play. This is totally normal behavior and does not automatically mean your dog has aggression issues. The truth is, sometimes it can be quite difficult to distinguish between play and aggression.

When your dog and another dog are playfully bowing and taking turns chasing, rolling over, and mouthing each other, these are all signs that they are engaging in play together. This type of play should be encouraged as it offers your dog valuable life experience and social lessons. This type of play helps your Portie practice his social skills and is a wonderful outlet for excess energy.

However, if the dogs are playing, but one or both seem stiff and tense, there may be more than a playful romp going on between them. Deep, drawn-out growling, staring into the other dog's eyes, and a one-sided chase may all be indications that one or both of the dogs are showing some real aggression, and you may need to end the encounter.

If you feel your Portie is playing too rough or becoming aggressive with you, simply walk away and ignore him. In a pack of dogs, older dogs will naturally teach the younger pups when enough is enough. They do this with a verbal cue and then end play immediately. Even puppies of the same litter do this to each other.

As the owner, you can take the same stance. When play becomes too rough, give a loud verbal "yip" and walk away, ignoring your dog. After a minute, once the dog seems to have shifted his attention, return to play. Repeat this process until the puppy understands that rough play is not acceptable. Eventually, he will understand the reason you keep walking

away and will lessen his intensity. After all, it was not his intent to harm you. He is still learning his boundaries.

Also, be aware of how you approach your dog for play. If you come in swinging and throwing your hands and arms around, this is encouraging your dog to play rough. Use toys instead of your body and keep movements gentle.

What to do When Pets Don't Get Along

If you've exhausted all the above tips and your pets simply can't seem to get along, call a professional and get help. Don't hesitate, as the situation could escalate quickly and lead to injury. The sooner you address the aggression with a trained professional, the easier it will be to overcome.

If you find yourself in a situation needing to break up a fight between dogs, you need to know how to do so safely so that you are not harmed in the process. Use the wheelbarrow method by grabbing each dog by the back legs and pulling them apart. You will need two people restraining the dogs for this method.

If you are alone, grab two metal pots and bang them against each other to make a loud noise. This should startle and distract the dogs long enough for you to separate them before the aggression continues. Water also works well to distract them. If you are outside, grab the hose and spray both dogs to distract them so you can separate them physically.

Never put yourself between two fighting dogs, no matter how much you trust them. This could likely lead to injury, even if they do not intend to cause you harm.

CHAPTER 9

Exercising Your Portuguese Water Dog

> PWDs need daily exercise. While walks are a good form of exercise, PWDs need to run as well. Playing fetch or Frisbee in the backyard is an excellent choice. This is a working breed and they do best when you give them a job, such as agility, obedience, tracking, and water work. These activities satisfy the need for both mental stimulation and exercise.
>
> JILL ROUDEBUSH
> *Maritimo Portuguese Water Dogs*

How Much Exercise Does a Portuguese Water Dog Need?

The Portuguese Water Dog has above-average exercise requirements and will need substantial physical activity to keep him busy. If you're looking for a dog that will happily lounge and hang out all day, the Portie is not the breed for you. After all, they were bred to work long days on fishing boats! A short daily walk will not suffice for this breed.

Though the Portuguese Water Dog requires an active lifestyle, it is important to note that when they are puppies, you must exercise them gently as their joints are not fully developed until the age of about 18 months. Swimming, gentle walks, and playtime are best for a puppy's developing joints. Hiking and jogging long distances are better suited for mature Porties.

> **66**
>
> *Walking and swimming are great forms of exercise, and I believe that PWDs need a time to run as well. Running uses different muscles than walking. It is very important that they get to run, even if you need to go to an open field and have them on a twenty-foot lead.*
>
> PATTI MCKNIGHT
> *McKnight's PWDs*
>
> **99**

Easy Ways to Stay Active

Making exercise fun and exciting not only helps your Portie get physical; it also stimulates him mentally. A swim, hike, or jog are all great ideas that a Portuguese Water Dog will love, but what about the days when those options aren't possible? Maybe the weather is poor, or an injury keeps you down temporarily. Try some of the following ideas to help you and your dog get past a rainy day or an exercise slump!

Use a Flirt Pole

A flirt pole is basically a stick with a toy attached to the end with a string. It allows you to engage your dog in a game of chase without much movement of your own. You can even use the flirt pole from a seated position. A flirt pole can be a perfect solution for owners who have limited mobility and cannot run alongside their dog. The flirt pole engages your dog mentally and physically—a win-win!

*Photo Courtesy of
Alex Korab*

Play Hide-and-Seek

Once your dog has mastered basic commands and can sit and stay, try engaging him in a game of hide-and-seek. Take your dog to a chosen location in the house and have him sit and stay where he is. Then go hide elsewhere in the house and call him when you are ready.

If your dog won't stay still long enough to allow you to hide, try giving him a treat that will take him half a minute or so to finish. Once he finishes, call out from your hiding place and see how long it takes your Portuguese Water Dog to find you. Keep giving him encouragement until he figures out where you are. The game is fun for you and him alike and is a great way to give your dog exercise on a rainy day!

Play Fetch

So simple, yet so effective. There is not much a dog loves more than a game of fetch. Play with a tennis ball, rope, or Frisbee. Mix it up to keep things interesting. Your Portie will love it! Teach your dog to return the item to your lap, and this game can be a consistently easy outlet for excess energy.

Scavenger Hunt

A typical dog has up to 300 million olfactory receptors in his nose, and the part of a dog's brain devoted to smell is proportionally 40 times larger than a human's. That means your Portuguese Water Dog has a powerful sniffer! Make mealtime or snack time fun by creating a game out of it and putting that nose to work.

Hide small amounts of food or treats around a room and see if your dog can sniff them out. If you hide them in enough areas, he may find himself running around the room from spot to spot, trying to find the sources of the smell. While this may not provide as much exercise as some of the previous suggestions, it is still a way to keep a bored dog entertained on a dreary day.

Dog Day Care

Even if you spend most of your time home with your dog, an occasional trip to a local dog day care is a great way to give your pup some playtime with other dogs while also allowing you to run errands without leaving your Portie alone. After a few hours at day care, your Portie will likely be ready for a relaxing nap at home.

> **"**
>
> *The best type of home for a PWD is one that wants and allows their PWD to be part of their family and participate in family activities, and not just be a spectator. A good example is a family that has children that participate in sports and takes their PWD with them to practices and games when it is appropriate. PWDs are not 'couch potato' types of dogs. They are a working breed and need and like to be busy.*
>
> PATTI MCKNIGHT
> *McKnight's PWDs*
>
> **"**

Importance of Mental Exercise

> *Mental exercise is just as important as physical exercise. This can be achieved through obedience training, but mind games, such as finding a treat hidden under a cup, or playing hide-and-seek with treats hidden outside or in different rooms, are also fun, brain-stimulating activities.*
>
> PATTI MCKNIGHT
> *McKnight's PWDs*

Physical exercise often gets all the attention, but mental exercise is just as important, especially for a highly intelligent dog like the Portuguese Water Dog. A bored Portuguese Water Dog can cause a lot of destruction! Many of the suggestions above serve as both mental and physical exercise. Playing hide-and-seek, doing scavenger hunts, and using a flirt pole all provide a high amount of direct mental stimulation, as does interacting with other dogs at dog day care. However, there are other things you can do with your Portie to stimulate him mentally as well.

Training your Portuguese Water Dog to learn a new trick is an excellent way to give him mental stimulation and strengthen your bond. Learning a new command will help to further build the relationship and trust between you two, resulting in a more obedient and willing dog. After he has mastered all the basic commands, get creative and teach your Portie some fun tricks like jumping through a hoop, walking backward, or crawling. You can even teach him to retrieve his toys by name and put them back in their designated places.

There are also toys and puzzles designed specifically for dogs, intended to exercise their mind. Kong makes a range of toys that can keep your dog occupied for a long time and are basically indestructible. A favorite is the Classic Dog Toy. This is a rubber toy with a hollow center made for stuffing with treats. Kong has a line of treats and snacks, or you can simply fill the toy with peanut butter. The Kong toys are dishwasher

Photo Courtesy of Chris and Jon Zombek

safe and cost between $8 and $25, depending on size, making them a great, affordable option.

Another option is a dog puzzle. The Trixie Poker Box has four compartments, all covered by a lid. Your dog must figure out how each lid can be removed to get the reward waiting inside. All four lids open differently, so this will take some real focus and determination on your dog's part. Once your Portie figures out the trick to opening all boxes,

HISTORICAL FACT

Messenger Dogs

Early Portuguese Water Dogs are believed to have carried messages between ships and even sailed with the Spanish Armada in 1588. According to legend, some of these excellent swimmers escaped the vessels of the Spanish Armada when the English defeated them and swam ashore to mingle with other dogs. Some believe that these early PWDs mated with local dogs and played a part in the early lineage of the Irish Water Spaniel and the Kerry Blue Terrier.

this puzzle may not present a challenge anymore. So, keep the toy in your arsenal for the occasional day when your dog must be left alone.

If you prefer a mentally stimulating toy without the use of treats, try getting your dog an Outward Hound Hide A Squirrel Puzzle Dog Toy. It's a hollow, plush tree stump with holes around it. Inside, there are three plush squirrels that squeak. Your dog will have tons of fun trying to pull the squirrels from the stump. This is a great option for a dog who may need to watch his weight, but it probably isn't a good idea for a vigorous chewer since the squirrels can be torn apart with enough effort. This toy may not last long, especially for an excitable Portuguese Water Dog.

Tips for a Bored Dog

These dogs naturally crave work and companion activities and will likely find trouble if left alone to entertain themselves. Do not get a Portuguese Water Dog if you plan to leave him alone often. However, every dog must be left alone for some periods of time occasionally. Try the mental stimulation tips above to keep him busy while you're away. Another option is an electronic device that you can control and interact with your dog through a mobile device, such as a phone.

Clever Pet is one of these devices. This is a unique system that challenges your dog with sequences, memory games, and electronically released treats or food when solved. This system comes with a light-up pad that shows different colors and patterns. Clever Pet is designed to progressively get more challenging as your dog figures it out. Use the mobile application to track progress and monitor use. This system is wonderful for dogs who are left alone for long periods of the day. It comes with a $250 price tag, but it is worth it if it means you don't have to spend money cleaning up after a bored dog.

If your Portuguese Water Dog loves a game of fetch, check out the iFetch Frenzy. Not as high-tech as the original iFetch, which is electronic and can launch a tennis ball up to 30 feet, the iFetch Frenzy uses gravity instead of electricity to drop the ball through one of three holes and send it rolling across the floor. Once your dog learns to return the ball to the top, he can play solo fetch for hours while you are away. Remember, these devices are not a substitution for exercise with you. Your Portie may enjoy these solo games occasionally, but he will thrive with companionship and side-by-side activity.

When you do have to leave your Portie alone for a time, rotate interactive toys that will help to keep him entertained while you are away. Some owners even like to leave the television on while they're gone. There are specific shows on DogTV that are geared specifically toward dogs, which some canines really seem to enjoy.

Photo Courtesy of
Bettina Landauer

CHAPTER 10

Training Your Portuguese Water Dog

Benefits of Proper Training

> "
>
> *Group obedience classes are wonderful for PWDs as puppies, but also as they get older. Many families feel that any obedience class past your typical puppy kindergarten is only for people that want to compete. That's just not true. There are so many great classes and activities that you can do without ever competing. A PWD was bred to be on a fishing boat with a fisherman, and the two worked in tandem throughout the day. Taking an obedience or agility class with your dog is not about earning a title, but about growing a similar bond with your dog.*
>
>
>
> CHRISTIE KELLO
> *Windward Portuguese Water Dogs*
>
> "
>

The benefits of training your Portuguese Water Dog are endless. Not only will it strengthen the relationship between you and him, but it will undoubtedly help keep your dog safe. A properly trained Portuguese Water Dog will come when called and will obey out of trust

Photo Courtesy of
Valerie Hawk

and loyalty. This is particularly important in emergency scenarios or times of crisis. Obedience may even save your dog's life.

There are options when it comes to training your Portie. You can attend a group obedience class, hire a personal dog trainer either at a facility or in your home, or do it yourself. No matter what you choose to do, be diligent and stick with a consistent training schedule. The rewards of an obedient dog will pay off for years to come.

Training at Home

Many people choose to train their dogs in their own home. Training your Portie yourself is possible and rewarding if you do it properly. Whether you train your Portuguese Water Dog yourself or you prefer to hire a professional trainer, training in your own home is a great way to fit training into even the busiest of schedules. Also, it allows you to begin training earlier and protect your young puppy from potential virus exposure in an obedience class.

Photo Courtesy of Nicole Sendar

There are drawbacks, however, to training at home. One is not seeing how your dog reacts in less-than-optimal situations. If all training takes place in the distraction-free zone of your home, your dog may not know how to react when there are distractions around. You need your dog to obey in any situation, at home or outside, where there are potentially dangerous distractions everywhere. In a group class setting, your dog is learning to be obedient regardless of what is going on around him, and this is an invaluable skill.

When training at home, it is good practice to occasionally take your dog somewhere else to practice obedience with real-life distractions. If you hire a trainer, ask how they make sure to train your dog in all situations and ask about the possibility of taking a training field trip to a public place. This option gives you the best of both worlds while also ensuring proper training.

> **"**
>
> *PWDs are way smart and have a bit of a stubborn streak. We believe they are critical thinkers and rarely take a simple 'no' for an answer. They have a great memory and will go back to something when you are not looking.*
>
> CATHERINE M. DUGAN
> *Aviator Kennels*
> **"**

Maintaining Clear Expectations

Regardless of whether you choose to train at home or in a group setting such as an obedience class, it's important you maintain clear expectations. This will set you and your Portie up for success from the beginning. Training a dog, even one as intelligent as a Portuguese Water Dog, is a lot of work and may test your patience at times. Persistence and positivity will pay off immensely.

If you choose to attend obedience classes, either private or group, there are a few things you should know ahead of time. These classes are usually held once or twice a week, and most facilities require you to provide vaccination records before classes begin. Obedience training typically begins at six months of age, but dog ages in a class can vary widely. It is never too late to start obedience training, so even if you have a senior Portie, he's not too old to learn!

Before your first training session, ask what is provided and if there is anything you should bring. The facility will likely require your dog to have a leash and may ask you to provide your own training treats. Most obedience classes require a name tag with identification, and some require a clicker. By purchasing all necessary supplies before the class, you can ensure that all your time is spent learning from the trainer and not scrambling to get what you need.

No matter how frequent obedient classes are, be prepared to spend a minimum of 15 to 20 minutes daily working on what your dog has learned. Just as with any skill, obedience training takes practice and repetition. Your Portuguese Water Dog is intelligent and independent, and he wants to please and obey you. Show him patience as he learns, and reinforce good behaviors positively.

Basic Commands

Obedience training is not just about learning to sit or shake; it's about building trust between you and your dog. Learning how to communicate your wishes in a way your dog can understand is the goal. A great way to build this trust is by teaching your dog basic commands. These basic commands lay the foundation for further training in the future.

Most obedience classes or personal trainers will begin the training by teaching a few easy, basic commands. If you are choosing to be the trainer yourself, follow the steps below to master these five basic commands.

Sit – The sit command is the easiest one to teach and can be learned in a short period of time. Take your dog to a calm area that is free of distractions like toys. Have a bag full of very small training treats ready. With your dog standing, facing you, hold a treat in front of his nose and slowly raise it up and over

FUN FACT
BARK

The Baseball Aquatic Retrieval Corps, or BARK, comprises an elite team of six Portuguese Water Dogs tasked with retrieving baseballs from McCovey Cove. These rogue balls, called "splash hits," are from Pacific Bell Park (now called Oracle Park) and are auctioned off to benefit a local organization called Pets in Need. Oracle Park is home to the San Francisco Giants and seats about 40,000 fans.

his head so that he is forced to sit down and look up. Give the verbal command "sit" as you do this. When he sits, reward him with a treat and a key phrase such as "yes" or "good." If you're training with a clicker, also give a click when he obeys the command.

Down

Once your dog has mastered the sit command, move on to the down command. Guide your dog into a seated position, facing you. Hold a treat in front of his nose, lower it to the floor, and give the verbal command "down." If your dog raises his backside to a standing position to retrieve the treat, take the treat away and say "no." Begin again from a seated position. When your dog successfully lies down to retrieve the treat, reward with a treat, a positive verbal cue such as "yes," and a click.

Heel

Teaching your dog to heel requires him to walk on your left side at your pace whenever you're out and about. The heel command is a bit challenging and requires significant focus from your dog. He must stop when you stop and walk when you walk, never stepping in front of your left heel. This command is great for preventing leash tugging.

Begin by having your dog sit in front, facing you. Using your left hand, let your dog smell the treat and then swing your arm around to the left, luring your dog to turn around and stop in a position next to you but slightly behind, facing the same direction you are. Reward your dog immediately when he arrives in the correct position. Use the command "heel." Repeat this command many times, always having your dog come to the heel position before rewarding him.

After your dog has mastered the heel position, progress by taking a few steps using the same verbal "heel" command. Reward your dog for walking with you in the correct position. If your dog leaves the correct heel position, guide him back to where he is supposed to be before continuing.

Stay

To teach your dog to stay, command him to sit, facing you. With a visible treat in hand, hold out your palm to your dog and say, "stay." Take one

step backward. If your dog doesn't move, quickly return to your dog and reward him. You don't want your dog leaving the stay position to retrieve the treat. If your dog moves, say "no" and return him to a sitting position. As your dog gets the hang of "stay," increase the number of steps.

Leave It

This command is valuable and can help keep your dog safe if he gets into something potentially dangerous. Begin with two treats, one in each hand. Keep one hand in a fist, but allow your dog to sniff the treat. As your dog tries to get into your hand to get the treat, verbally command him to "leave it." Repeat this command until your dog backs off, and then reward with the treat from the other hand. As your dog progresses, make the treat more accessible and challenge your pup to leave it in exchange for another treat.

Methods of Training

There are two main methods when it comes to training a dog: alpha dog training and positive reinforcement. Hotly debated among dog trainers, these two methods are vastly different. When choosing the method that is right for your dog, you must take some things into consideration and understand the details of each one.

> **"**
>
> *When it comes to training, PWDs' intelligence is what makes them so unique. They are very easy to train, and they have such a wonderful willingness to learn and work. If owners put the time into training their dog, they will experience the most beautiful bond with a dog that they have ever experienced. They can also expect a very loyal and well-behaved companion.*
>
> JILL ROUDEBUSH
> *Maritimo Portuguese Water Dogs*
>
> **"**

Alpha Dog Training

Alpha training, popularized by television dog trainer Cesar Millan, focuses on making yourself the alpha or the leader of the pack. This training begins early by maintaining heavy control over your dog's actions. Users of this method are told to never allow their dog in their bed, not to let a dog go through a doorway before they do, and never to get down at eye level with the dog. It is also advised that people touch their dog's food to get their scent on it before giving it to him and not to let the dog eat until the owner gives the verbal okay.

Proponents of this method claim that dogs are pack animals and need to have a sense of who is alpha in order to learn to submit. They claim that wolves will assert their dominance over one another to keep each other in check, and they attempt to achieve the same assertion by using highly controversial methods. However, research has shown that wolves in the

Photo Courtesy of Bettina Landauer

wild actually do not have such a rigid hierarchy. They live socially among each other, much like humans do with our own families. Also, cross-species dominance has not proven successful at any point in history.

When it comes to obedience training, alpha training employs the use of restraints such as choke and shock collars and forceful body maneuvers. This method relies heavily on punishments and teaching your dog what he is doing wrong rather than teaching him how to do it right. While some trainers believe in the effectiveness of alpha training methods, others believe it is cruel and can undermine your relationship with your dog, making it one based on fear and not trust. This method of training is absolutely not suitable for a Portuguese Water Dog.

Positive Reinforcement

The most widely accepted and recommended method of training today is positive reinforcement. The idea is that by reinforcing good behavior and obedience with desirable treats and praise, your dog will learn the commands and build trust with the trainer. It is still important to let your dog know that you are in control, but this is done through positive reinforcement rather than force. Bad behavior is not punished by harm or discomfort; rather, it is ignored or redirected until the positive behavior becomes consistent. It is about helping your dog understand what you want him to do so he can do it.

Dogs have been selectively bred over thousands of years to live alongside humans. They thrive on companionship and will typically do anything to please their people. Using positive reinforcement is a method of teaching them to understand what you want them to do and teaching them that what makes you happy also makes them happy. This is the opposite of fear-based training and will build loyalty and trust naturally.

When training using the positive reinforcement method, there are two types of reinforcements used: primary and secondary.

> **"**
>
> *They are what I refer to as 'soft spirits': If they are yelled at or harshly reprimanded, they seem to get their feelings hurt, so after a good correction they need to be touched and loved. This helps them to understand that they are loved, but that their unwanted actions are not acceptable.*
>
> PATTI MCKNIGHT
> *McKnight's PWDs*
>
> **"**

Primary Reinforcement – Primary reinforcements are directly related to the innate basic needs your dog has. These include things such as food and water. Training treats are a primary reinforcement successfully used in training. Make sure you use specific training treats, as they are typically small so that your dog can train with them longer without being overfed. Many trainers also use small bits of deli meat as a high-value reward.

> **"**
> *In training my PWDs, I have found that it's only after repeating things three times that I get results. The fourth time, they look at me like, 'What's wrong with you! We just did this!'*
>
> PATTI MCKNIGHT
> *McKnight's PWDs*
> **"**

Secondary Reinforcement – Secondary reinforcements are things not based on instinctual, basic needs but, rather, are cultural constructs. This includes verbal praise, smiles, and pats. Your dog must learn to associate these actions positively by pairing them with primary reinforcements.

Another type of secondary reinforcement is conditioned reinforcement. This is when something neutral, such as a whistle or a clicker, is used in conjunction with a primary reinforcement to create a positive association. Conditioned reinforcements can be highly effective initially but can lose their effectiveness when the primary reinforcement is taken away for an extended period.

Dangers of Negative Reinforcement

> **"**
> *Clicker training and other positive reinforcement methods are ideal for a PWD. One should avoid all aversive methods, such as choke collars, electric shock collars, prong collars, noise makers, scat mats, and electronic fencing. This breed is smart and wants to please. They need gentle training methods and can be easily ruined by punitive approaches to training.*
>
> CHERYL W. HOOFNAGLE
> *Blue Run Portuguese Water Dogs*
> **"**

Correcting by punishment, as is used in alpha training, has no scientific research backing it up as a legitimate training method. This type of forced control over a dog can lead to fear and anxiety and can even put you or your family in danger. Using this method without an experienced professional's supervision can lead to a damaged relationship with your dog and a loss of trust.

Not only is this type of training risky, but it is also often ineffective. Your dog almost never does anything "bad" intentionally. He is aiming to please, and if he is disobedient, it is most likely because he has not been taught what he is supposed to do. By punishing your dog when he does something undesirable, he will often be hurt and confused by what has happened. He may never fully understand which action was the reason for his discomfort in the first place.

Instead of punishing your dog to stop him from doing what he isn't supposed to, show him what he is supposed to do and reward him for that. It may take a little bit longer to master, but your relationship will grow positively in the process.

When to Hire a Trainer

If you are attempting to train at home but aren't making progress, it may be time to hire a professional trainer. Training a dog takes a lot of time and consistency, and it is easy to get frustrated, sending your dog mixed messages while training. If the mixed signals go on for too long, it can cause major setbacks in your dog's progress. If you are dealing with any kind of aggression or poor social behaviors that do not seem to be improving with work, hire a trainer specialized in that area to help you get through to your dog. If you think you need help from a professional trainer—don't put it off. The sooner your dog is properly trained, the sooner you can live together in peaceful companionship.

CHAPTER 11

Traveling with Your Portuguese Water Dog

> *Mine are always in a crate when I'm driving. It's safer for me and for them. Ginger-type cookies can help with throwing up or, if possible, do not feed them within an hour before traveling. Mine will whine if they need to go potty, but otherwise they ride and travel well.*
>
> PATTI MCKNIGHT
> *McKnight's PWDs*

Some people love to travel, and when they do, they love the idea of taking their four-legged companion with them! However, traveling isn't quite as easy for your Portie as it is for you. This chapter will look at all the ins and outs of traveling with your Portuguese Water Dog and prepare you with the knowledge to help you make the best decision for you and your dog.

Flying with Your Dog

Flying with your Portuguese Water Dog will take significant planning beforehand. There are only so many pets allowed on each airplane (this varies by airline and size of the plane), so book your flight as early as possible to obtain a spot. In the past, airlines treated cargo animals just like any other luggage. Dogs were often left traumatized and sometimes even died because of uncontrolled temperatures, lack of water, etc. Luckily, today, airlines have implemented regulations to keep animals housed in the cargo area as safe and happy as possible.

Your dog will most likely not be allowed to fly in the passenger area due to his size

HISTORICAL FACT

On the Brink of Extinction

Now one of the top 50 breeds registered with the AKC, Portuguese Water Dogs faced extinction nearly 100 years ago. In the 1930s, a wealthy Portuguese fisherman named Vasco Bensaude sought to re-establish this breed. His most prolific stud dog, named Leao, lived from 1930 to 1942. This breed likely came to America in the 1950s and was first recognized by the AKC in 1983.

but instead will have to be checked into the cargo area in a crate. Most airlines charge a fee for transporting animals. It is usually somewhere between $75 and $200 each way. If possible, get a direct flight for you and your dog.

If you're flying with a very young Portie, you may be able to have him in the cabin with you on a flight. Typically the weight limit for pets in the cabin is 20—25 pounds, but every airline's rules and regulations are a little different. Check with your preferred airline before making plans. If your puppy is able to fly as a carry-on, he will likely have to remain in an airline-approved crate that is able to fit under the seat, approximately 17.5 inches by 12 inches by 7.5 inches tall. These can be a hard or soft shell, but it should be sturdy and well-ventilated.

According to the American Kennel Club, "The Federal Aviation Administration considers the pet-travel crate to be carry-on luggage, and it must be put through the carry-on luggage screening device – but your puppy does not. When you go through security, carry the pup in your arms and take him through the human screening process."

While you may want to take your sweet Portie with you wherever you go, flying isn't a fun thing for dogs and does cause them stress. No matter how much airlines have worked to improve the process for animals, air travel will still be traumatizing for your dog and does carry a bit of risk.

Guidelines for flying animals vary greatly based on the airline, so be sure to check with your specific airline before traveling. Some require a certificate of veterinary inspection (CVI) before flying. Make sure you do thorough research on each airline and choose the one you think suits your Portie's needs best. Choosing the right airline can make or break your traveling experience.

When it comes to airline-approved kennels, regulations are constantly changing. Check your local airline for current recommendations on preferred kennels and read consumer reviews. Choosing a safe and sturdy kennel for your Portuguese Water Dog is one of the most important decisions you will make when deciding to fly with your dog. It will protect and keep him safe while travel is underway.

According to American Airlines, a kennel must be rigid, made from metal, plastic, or wood, and with no damage or cracks evident. It must be well-ventilated on three or four sides, and it must have a metal door. Collapsible kennels are prohibited. Depending on the type of flight or plane, there may be size requirements for the kennel, so call your airline for specifics.

Most airlines will allow you to attach a bag of food that may be used in case of delay. Some even allow a drip water dispenser for your dog on the flight, so it's important you let your dog practice with one of these before the flight if he is unfamiliar.

Many airlines will also allow a small blanket or piece of clothing in the crate with your scent to bring your dog comfort. So if this is an option, utilize it! Most airlines have banned crate pads, toys, bones, or treats, as well as newspaper, straw, or hay bedding. Most also do not allow any collar other than a flat collar, meaning muzzles, shock collars, and metal collars are prohibited. Sending medication with your dog is also not allowed. Because each airline is different, confirm with your specific airline before you plan.

Because your Portuguese Water Dog will have to be checked in with the luggage, it would be wise to arrive as close to flight time as possible so he does not have a long wait without you. Take your Portie out to potty just before you leave for the airport, as grass is often difficult to find once you enter the airport property. If you have the opportunity, allow your dog to relieve himself just before entering the building as well. It is also wise to withhold food and water for a few hours before traveling so that your dog does not become sick on the flight.

Other Methods of Transportation

If traveling from city to city, you may consider a train. Unfortunately, dogs over 20 pounds are not allowed on Amtrak, which means your mature Portie will not be accommodated. If you are traveling with a very young Portuguese Water Dog under 20 pounds, know that dogs are not allowed on trips over seven hours, including loading time. Also, availability is limited for pets, so book early.

The fee for traveling with your pup on Amtrak is $26—far cheaper than air travel. If you choose to travel by train, check the latest kennel regulations to make sure you are in compliance.

Most bus lines do not allow larger dogs to ride unless they are service dogs. However, all bus lines are different, so check with your local bus service to find out if they allow dogs.

Hotel Stays and House Rentals

> **"**
>
> *Take your own water bowl and water (strange water can upset a dog's stomach and cause soft stools). Take a sheet or blanket to throw over hotel beds. Always take a crate, and do not leave your dog loose in a hotel room. Take toys and a leash. And always clean up after your dog defecates!*
>
> ROBIN L. BURMEISTER
> *Windward Portuguese Water Dogs*
>
> **"**

Before planning overnight travel with your Portie, make sure you have hotel arrangements ahead of time if needed. Not all hotels are pet friendly, and even those that claim to be may have breed and size restrictions. Before booking, call and check their pet policy and make sure they will allow your Portuguese Water Dog to stay. Sometimes a hotel booking website will list a hotel as "pet friendly," but this doesn't always mean your dog can stay with you, so call ahead and get the details so that there aren't any surprises when you arrive.

Another thing to consider when choosing a hotel is whether or not it has adequate outdoor space. Even some "pet-friendly" hotels aren't actually convenient for pets, as there is no space to walk your dog or let him do his business. Be sure to request a room on the ground floor so that you don't have to take the stairs or elevator every time your dog needs to go outside.

Some hotels reserve old, outdated rooms for pets, so call and check ahead of time to see if the pet rooms are different from the other rooms. Even if you don't anticipate using it, bring a kennel to the hotel in case you must leave your dog unattended. You never know when an emergency will happen, and it's better to be prepared.

These same principles apply to Airbnb and VRBO rentals as well. Double-check that a property is Portie-friendly and has adequate accommodations and outdoor space before you book.

*Photo Courtesy of
Bettina Landauer*

When to Leave Your Portuguese Water Dog Behind

As we've discussed, traveling with your Portuguese Water Dog may not be as simple as you wish. Often it causes distress and puts your dog in less-than-ideal situations. Even if you want to take him along, it may be wise to know when to leave him behind. There are several options for dog care while you're away that are not only safe but are sometimes downright fun for your dog!

Kenneling vs. Dog Sitting

There are two basic choices for care while you are gone. You can put your dog at a boarding kennel until you return, or you can hire a dog sitter. Depending on your needs and the personality of your dog, either of these can be a great option. You can also ask a family member or friend to care for your dog while you are away. Just be sure they are responsible and care for your Portie as much as you do!

If you won't be gone for an extended period, you might find hiring a dog sitter a more affordable option. This is typically when you hire someone to come and take your dog out two to three times a day and make sure he has food and water. You might hire a professional dog sitter or a trusted friend or family member. Because Portuguese Water Dogs require so much exercise, this is only a good option for a day or two. After this, your dog may begin to feel cooped up and anxious, likely becoming destructive.

You can also hire a 24-hour dog sitter who will stay overnight to care for your dog. This will, of course, be a more expensive option. It would allow your dog to have companionship and constant care, however, which is something your Portuguese Water Dog would enjoy.

A boarding kennel is likely the best option for your Portie if he is well-socialized and gets along well with other dogs. Most of these places allow your dog to play with other dogs in a safe environment for most of the day. A stay at a boarding kennel can be like a vacation for your dog!

Photo Courtesy of Nancy Puskorius

Every boarding facility is different and enforces its own unique rules and policies. The accommodations range from basic kennels to full-sized rooms with elevated dog beds and doggy doors to a private patio. Many even have cameras set up so you can check in on your dog from your phone.

Frequently, quality boarding facilities will have a common area inside and out where dogs can play and romp. The cost per night varies greatly depending on location and amenities.

Every quality kennel will require a Bordetella vaccine before your dog's stay. Never take your dog to a place that doesn't ask for this. Bordetella is highly contagious and common, and it only takes one dog to cause an outbreak that makes your dog sick. Plan for your dog to get the vaccine a minimum of two weeks before his stay.

Ask around among other dog owners and check reviews before you choose a place to take your dog while you're away. You don't want to take your Portuguese Water Dog just anywhere. Be sure you can trust that they will provide adequate care and interaction so that you can spend your trip having fun and not worrying about your Portie!

Bonus Tips and Tricks for Traveling

66

Plan stops in areas not frequented by other dogs to avoid exposure to parasites and viruses. Make sure your vehicle is sufficiently cool where your crate will be. Provide a fan if your vehicle does not have air vents in the crate area.

MARLENE NICEWANDER
Cove's End Portuguese Water Dogs

99

Traveling with your Portuguese Water Dog can be fun and exciting, but it can also be stressful! Follow these tips to help any trip with your loyal companion be a stress-free one!

- Don't feed your dog within four hours of any trip. This includes car rides, plane rides, and any other method of transportation. This may help prevent you from having to clean up vomit.
- Exercise your Portie vigorously the day before and the day of your trip. Let him get as much energy out as he possibly can before being put into his crate.
- Don't sedate your dog! This once-common practice is no longer recommended by veterinarians. Sedating a dog can inhibit his ability to react in an emergency and is simply not good for his health.
- Check in as late as possible at the airport so that your dog doesn't have to spend extra time waiting.
- If you are flying, make sure that your rental car or car service allows for dogs to ride.
- Always have a bowl, leash, water, and plastic waste bags with you. No matter how you are traveling, these basic items will be daily necessities. If you're driving, use a safety harness, as discussed earlier, and stop often to let your dog potty and drink water.
- Always have the number of a local emergency vet on hand. Emergencies can happen anywhere, so look up local animal hospitals before you travel—just in case!

CHAPTER 12

Grooming Your Portuguese Water Dog

> *Daily grooming is a learned process. Start when pup is first home and get him used to a grooming table. The Portuguese Water Dog Club of America provides a schematic about grooming, and we always provide referrals for PWD-friendly groomers in their area.*
>
> CATHERINE M. DUGAN
> *Aviator Kennels*

The Grooming Needs of a Portuguese Water Dog

A Portuguese Water Dog is a showstopper on the street with his luscious curls and waves. Due to his single-layer, non-shedding coat, the Portuguese Water Dog requires a great deal of coat care. Everyone loves a hypoallergenic dog, but along with that benefit comes the requirement to maintain that beautiful hair!

Plan to spend anywhere from $60 to $100 every six weeks having your Portie professionally groomed. Because of his non-shedding coat, your Portie will need a full haircut every month and a half at minimum to maintain his coat and prevent matting and other issues. Invest in a good-quality slicker brush, and use it at least twice a week to keep the coat free of mats in between cuts.

> **"**
>
> *I like to have the muzzle shaved. It looks neater and helps with keeping excess water off the face. I also like to see the ears trimmed to the ear leather. PWDs have a half-heart-like shape to the bottom of their ears; it's a distinctive look for a PWD that is nice to enhance.*
>
> PATTI MCKNIGHT
> *McKnight's PWDs*
> **"**

Coat Basics

A Portie will have one of two coat types: one is wavy and loose, and the other is short, tight curls. According to Christie Kello from Windward Portuguese Water Dogs in Ohio, "There is a common misconception that [Porties are] 'hypoallergenic' and [they] don't lose hair. A Portuguese Water Dog loses hair just like a person." This means your Portie will need regular clips to keep his hair trimmed and tangle-free.

Though a groomer will clip your dog however you choose, there are two common haircuts for the Portuguese Water Dog.

Photo Courtesy of Nancy Puskorius

The Retriever Clip: This is one of the classic hairstyles for the Portie. The whole coat is trimmed evenly down to about an inch, with some rounding at the feet. The muzzle and ears are also cut short, and the head blends with the body, except for an acceptable dome shape at the top. There is long hair left at the end of the tail.

The Lion Clip: For this clip, the back half of the dog is clipped very short, except for the end of the tail, which is left long. The hair on the front of the body is left at a longer length, usually several inches, resembling that of a lion's mane. This cut is a head-turner but does require more maintenance.

Grooming Tools

If you choose to handle some of the grooming yourself, invest in quality pet shampoo and conditioner and aim to bathe your Portie once every month or so. This will help keep the coat clean and prevent cobweb matting at the skin.

The choice of shampoo is based on your personal preference, so you may have to try a few out before finding one that is right for you and your dog. Whichever shampoo you choose, make sure it is free from parabens, dyes, sulfates, and DEA. These are ingredients commonly used in commercial shampoos but are known to have potentially damaging effects over time. It is also best to avoid any added fragrances, especially if your dog has sensitive skin.

Finding a grooming brush for your dog can easily become overwhelming because there are so many types of brushes, all created for different purposes and coat types. Since Porties are prone to tangles and mats, you will want to purchase a slicker brush. These are usually flat with short, fine, wire bristles. The slicker brush is used for removing mats and tangles. You may also want to purchase a natural bristle brush as a finishing brush. These brushes have tightly packed natural bristles and help to stimulate the skin's oils, keeping your dog's coat shiny and healthy.

Aside from coat care, you will also need to have nail trimmers, styptic powder, a dog toothbrush, toothpaste, and ear wash.

Bathing and Brushing

Marlene Nicewander from Coves End PWD in North Carolina says,

> 66
>
> *Brushing the surface of the coat is not adequate. You should be able to comb through the coat from the skin up. Mats can be painful, [so] break them up and comb out mats. Take your puppy on a regular schedule to the groomer and do the pup's nails weekly.*
>
> 99

As mentioned before, regular brushing and baths are the keys to keeping your Portuguese Water Dog clean and his coat healthy. You shouldn't bathe your dog more than once a month as this can strip the oils from his skin and cause dryness.

It is good practice to use a blow dryer to blow any excess dirt or hair off your Portie's coat before getting him in the bath. Keep the dryer far enough off the coat to avoid causing tangles. After this, proceed with shampooing your dog.

When shampooing your dog, use quality dog shampoo. If you are unsure of what to use, ask local vets and groomers what they recommend. Never use human shampoo or conditioner on your dog. It is best

to do this in a tub with a hand sprayer, but a large rinsing cup will do if that is all you have.

Make sure you clean the coat all the way down to the skin. Rinse with cool water and then use a towel to blot dry. Don't use the towel to rub your dog dry because this will cause tangles and mats to form in the coat.

Finish drying with a hair dryer and use the bristle brush to remove any tangles. Once finished, check the consistency of the coat with your hands. If one area feels denser, go back over that area with the brush to remove any mats.

Nail Trimming

Some people choose to have a groomer or a veterinarian trim their dog's nails for them, but you can easily do this at home with the right tools. You will need to invest in a quality nail trimmer. There are several types to choose from, but they will all get the job done, so choose based on your preference and what is easiest for you to maneuver.

You should also purchase some styptic powder. This will stop any bleeding if you accidentally cut a nail too short. Most clippers will come with instructions on how to clip the nails, and it is important to follow them carefully to avoid injury to your dog.

If you wait until your dog is older to begin trimming the nails, he will likely be leery of the strange tool in your hand. Introduce the nail clippers to your Portie early and often, even if he doesn't need a nail trim, so he can become accustomed to the tool.

Let your dog explore and sniff the trimmers so he can feel comfortable with it. Practice holding them near his feet to show him that they are not a threat. Reward him with treats to create a positive association. This will lay the groundwork for easy nail trims in the future!

A dog's nail is made up of the nail and the quick. The quick is the pink part inside the nail. If your dog has light-colored nails, the quick may be visible, making it easier to avoid. If the nails are black, you will not be able to see the quick and will need to be extra cautious not to trim too far back. If you do hit the quick, this is called quicking and is a very painful experience for your dog. It will bleed a lot, so immediately apply styptic powder.

The two most common types of nail trimmers are the guillotine type and the scissor type. To use the guillotine or scissor trimmers, carefully place the dog's nail into the clipper and cut at a 45-degree angle away from the pad. Remember, the longer a dog's nails, the longer the blood supply is inside the nail, so only trim a little at a time, even if your dog's nails are overgrown. As the nail is trimmed shorter, the blood supply will also retreat, making it possible to shorten his nails over time. Trim a small amount every ten days or so until they are the length you want. If you do cause bleeding, stop it immediately with styptic powder.

Cleaning the Eyes and Ears

> *Excess hair in the ears needs to be removed (ear canals need to breathe!), and eye crusties can be kept to a minimum by using a dab of Vaseline or baby oil in the corners of the eyes. You can then easily remove eye 'goobers' with a tissue.*
>
> ROBIN L. BURMEISTER
> *Windward Portuguese Water Dogs*

Along with coat care, ear and eye care are crucial parts of grooming that a Portuguese Water Dog needs. This breed tends to have quite a bit of hair in and around their ears, so you will need to clean your dog's ears out every week to get out trapped debris and waxy buildup. To do this, gently squeeze cleaning solution into one ear as directed on the bottle. Massage the ear canal and then move on to the other ear. Unless your Portie is particularly cooperative, you will need someone to help you hold your dog while you put the liquid in his ear.

You may also find you need to lightly trim the hair around your Portie's eyes between trips to the groomer. The hair on his face can quickly become long enough to impede his vision and trap dirt and debris in the area. To do this, very carefully trim the hair back with a pair of shears. If you do not think you can do this safely at home, ask your groomer to trim it every two to three weeks.

Dental Care

Dental health is often overlooked when it comes to dogs, but proper oral care is important! Dogs can suffer from the same oral diseases and pains that humans do. Your dog should be taken to the vet every year or two for a professional dental cleaning. Talk to your vet about how often he or she recommends.

FUN FACT

Breed Standard

PWDs can have a curly or wavy coat, according to the AKC's breed standard. Dogs competing in conformation events (competitive events for pure-bred PWDs) must have either a lion or retriever clip. A lion clip features a trimmed muzzle and hindquarters, with the hair at the end of the tail and front of the body left long. A retriever clip is designed to look more natural, with a short coat of hair all over the dog's body, no longer than an inch.

At home, brush your dog's teeth often with a dog-specific toothpaste to prevent any oral issues down the road. Never use human toothpaste, which is full of additives that are meant to be spat out and not swallowed. Brush gently and take it slow until your dog is accustomed to the toothbrush. If your dog is wary, begin by putting dog toothpaste on your finger and in your dog's mouth. Slowly work your way up to rubbing the toothbrush on his lips and eventually against his teeth. It is a good idea to do this at the same time you brush his coat every week to create a routine.

Brushing is not the only way to help your Portie keep his teeth in tip-top shape. Chewing has been shown to naturally reduce plaque and tartar buildup. Dental chews come in many sizes, so just make sure you get the right size for your dog. When using these, it is advisable to have your dog on your lap and hold one end of the chew in your hand as he enjoys the chomping. This will ensure that your precious pup does not try to swallow a piece that is too big for him and might cause choking.

How to Clip at Home

Clipping a Portuguese Water Dog at home is no easy job. If you plan to embark on the endeavor, arm yourself with the proper tools and setup, as mentioned above, to make the grooming session much easier for both you and your dog. Grooming a dog takes a great deal of skill and practice, so don't expect a show-quality result if you've never done it before.

At-home grooming sessions for a dog like the Portuguese Water Dog often take hours. It is not quite as easy as the trained professionals make it look! Seek instruction from videos online if you are set on doing it yourself, but do this before you have your dog ready to groom, as his patience may only last so long.

When to Seek Professional Help

Maintaining your Portuguese Water Dog's coat properly is so important to his health and overall care. If you find yourself unable to care for his coat in the way he needs, there is no shame in hiring a professional groomer for regular baths and clips. Never neglect your Portie's grooming needs, as the coat can get out of hand quickly and become a much tougher job.

CHAPTER 13

Basic Health Care

Veterinary Care

Your Portuguese Water Dog should see the vet routinely for check-ups and vaccinations. These appointments typically happen yearly unless there is a reason to come in more frequently. At these yearly check-ups, the vet will give your dog a good look-over to make sure things are functioning properly. The vet should listen to the heart and lungs and examine the ears, eyes, nose, and mouth. The visit should also include an abdominal examination, looking for any abnormalities. The vet may draw blood to check for heartworms and take a stool sample to check for other parasites. Sometimes the vet will examine your dog's gait and coat condition.

While you may think these appointments are unnecessary, Portuguese Water Dogs, like most purebred dogs, are susceptible to a few genetic conditions. These annual visits with your vet may allow you to catch any issues early before they become bigger.

Fleas and Ticks

Fleas are a common parasite that plague dogs, and they are a problem almost everywhere in the world. These tiny parasites reproduce quickly, with a female flea laying 20 to 40 eggs a day. This means a single flea in your home can quickly turn into an infestation that can be difficult to get rid of.

Ticks largely go unnoticed by their host, but they can cause a much bigger health problem than fleas. Ticks are notorious for transmitting dangerous diseases to dogs, humans, and other animals. Although ticks prefer a dog over a human, they will latch on to you if given the opportunity. For this reason, it is important to keep your dog protected from ticks at all times.

Flea and tick prevention are important for your Portie's health and for your own. There are many options when it comes to prevention. Understanding the benefits and the disadvantages of each one will allow you to choose which is best for your dog.

Topical flea and tick preventative medication is common and easily accessible without a prescription. Typically, this medication comes in a small tube that the owner squeezes onto the dog's back between the shoulder blades. This topical medication usually takes about 12 hours

*Photo Courtesy of
Justin J Derevyanik*

to take effect and will last about 30 days before it needs to be reapplied. This works because the solution is absorbed into the skin and circulates through the dog's bloodstream, treating fleas and ticks over the entire body, not just the area it was directly applied.

One disadvantage of this application is it usually leaves a greasy spot on your dog's back for a few days. Considering this is a medication, it's not something you want to touch yourself or allow children to come in contact with. There is usually a minimum age requirement for these medications, so it is best to consult your vet before applying them to a young Portie pup.

Another method of administration is oral medication. There are numerous tablets on the market that prevent fleas and ticks for 30 days. Some of these prevent heartworms and internal parasites as well. Depending on how your dog takes medication, this could be an easier way to prevent the parasites without the mess of topical medication. Just as with any medication, side effects do exist. While they are generally mild, some dogs can react with skin irritations, vomiting, or diarrhea.

You can also buy a special flea collar for your dog. These are collars worn in addition to your dog's identification collar. They are covered with topical flea medications, usually permethrin. This provides up to eight months of protection for your dog but can also cause skin irritation. While these collars have been deemed safe for dogs, permethrin can cause toxicity in cats. Just like with topical medication, children and adults should avoid contact with the active ingredients on flea collars. As with topical medications, flea collars should never be used on a young puppy, and the same precautions should be taken.

Even a dog that lives primarily indoors should be on a flea and tick preventative. It only takes one exposure to one of these parasites to potentially spell bad news for you and your dog. It is much better to take preventative measures than to have to deal with fleas or ticks after they have hitched a ride into your home.

If you suspect your dog might have fleas, you can purchase a flea comb at any pet store. Flea combs have very fine and closely spaced teeth that fleas cannot pass between. Run the flea comb over your dog's body at a 45-degree angle, focusing on the head, neck, and hindquarters, where fleas often congregate. If you see a flea in the comb, cover it quickly and trap it in a wet paper towel. Drop the flea in a bowl of soapy water to kill it.

You may give your dog a flea bath with a medicated shampoo, but mild dish soap is also proven effective at killing adult fleas without the harmful ingredients in a flea shampoo. Flea baths are only effective at killing adult fleas and are ineffective at killing larvae and eggs. This means they are a temporary solution, and as the larvae mature and the eggs hatch, the fleas will reappear on your Portie.

Once you have addressed the fleas on your Portuguese Water Dog, shift the focus to your home, as there may be fleas lurking there as well, waiting to re-infest your dog. Vacuum your entire house from the floor to the curtains. Anything upholstered is potentially a place where a flea has laid eggs. If you notice fleas in your home, continue vacuuming twice a day for two weeks in order to get rid of all the fleas as they hatch. Fleas reproduce quickly, so don't skip a day!

Ticks

Ticks and fleas are often treated using the same medication, as discussed in the previous section. Make sure your dog's preventative covers both fleas and ticks to help your Portuguese Water Dog avoid serious infection and disease.

Aside from medication, take care to avoid tall grass or brush, as this is where ticks are likely to be. If your dog does go through brush or tall grass, inspect him promptly when you get home and remove any ticks you find with the following steps.

1. With gloves on, use tweezers to grab the tick firmly and as close to the skin as possible.
2. Once you securely have the tick, pull straight up so none of the tick's mouthparts are left behind, causing infection.
3. Put the tick in a jar of soapy water to kill it, and clean the tick bite area thoroughly with antiseptic.
4. Keep the tick for identification purposes in the event your dog begins showing symptoms. These may take up to two weeks to present, so watch your Portie closely for changing behavior.

HEALTH ALERT!
GM-1 Storage Disease

GM-1 Storage Disease, or ganglio-sidosis, is a genetic disorder affecting a dog's metabolism. When a dog suffers from this disease, it cannot metabolize certain substances, which can build up in the dog's brain. Portuguese Water Dog breeders should screen for this disease and have a puppy's parents' genetic testing results available for review. Symptoms of GM-1 Storage Disease include lethargy, deafness, and coordination issues. Unfortunately, there is no known treatment for this condition.

Though both ticks and fleas can be seasonal in many regions, most vets recommend keeping your dog on a year-round preventative. Ticks can often go unnoticed by their host, but they pose a significant health risk to both you and your Portie. The following is a list of some serious diseases notoriously spread by ticks.

Lyme Disease

This common tick-borne disease carries serious risks for both humans and dogs. Transmitted by the black-legged tick, also called the deer tick, this disease is present across the United States, but it is more prevalent in the northeast.

Lyme Disease in dogs presents much like it does in humans, with flu-like symptoms, such as fever, chills, aches, and swollen lymph nodes. These signs can be difficult to detect in dogs, so watch for any change in behavior, apparent discomfort, or loss of appetite. If caught early, Lyme Disease can typically be treated successfully with an antibiotic, but prompt treatment is a must, so do not delay treatment.

If your vet suspects Lyme Disease, he will perform a C6 test to detect antibodies. This disease cannot be passed from an infected dog to a human or another dog. It can only be transmitted via tick bite.

Anaplasma

Symptoms of anaplasma are similar to Lyme Disease but also include low platelets, which is usually evident by unusual bleeding or bruising. This disease is typically found in the northeast United States, the upper Midwest, and the western coastal states.

Canine Ehrlichiosis

This tick-borne illness is found all over the world. Symptoms include loss of appetite, low platelets, and fever. If you notice your Portie is unwell after a tick bite, take him to the vet promptly to avoid chronic symptoms that are difficult to manage.

Rocky Mountain Spotted Fever

This is another common tick-borne disease that affects both humans and animals. It is typically found in ticks around the United States and in Central and South America. Symptoms of Rocky Mountain Fever are similar to others and include fever, loss of appetite, joint pain, low platelets, swollen lymph nodes, and occasionally neurological signs.

Babesiosis

Babesiosis can cause hemolysis, a breakdown of red blood cells, causing symptoms like jaundice, pale gums, dark urine, lethargy, depression, and sometimes, enlargement of the spleen. This disease can be fatal, so seek care for your Portie immediately.

Worms and Other Parasites

Worms and parasites are common in dogs, but they can become harmful if left untreated. These common worms and parasites include hookworm, ringworm, roundworms, tapeworms, whipworms, coccidia, giardia, and spirochetes. These parasites are typically diagnosed via a stool sample, but there are some signs and symptoms you can watch for as well.

Hookworm

Hookworm larvae live in the soil and can be picked up through common activities, such as walking through a park. These worms attach themselves to the intestinal walls and feed off your dog's blood. Diarrhea and weight loss are possible signs of hookworms.

Once your vet confirms a diagnosis, oral medication can be used to treat the parasite. Depending on the severity of the infestation, iron

supplements may be needed to treat anemia. Young puppies are most susceptible to hookworms, as is the case with most parasites.

Ringworm

This is actually a fungus and not a worm. Ringworm causes circular bald patches on your dog's skin and is easily spread from dog to dog and even dog to human in some cases. Your vet will probably treat your dog with a medicated shampoo and an oral medication.

Roundworm

Roundworms are common and typically discovered when the owner spots round white worms in a dog's stool. These worms are typically an inch or two in length. Other symptoms of roundworm include coughing, vomiting, and diarrhea; however, these only present in severe cases. Ringworms can also be passed to humans, especially kids.

Tapeworm

Tapeworm is commonly caused by ingesting larvae, typically by eating a flea. Weight loss and diarrhea are common symptoms, as well as small worm segments in your dog's stool. These often resemble grains of rice. Treatment includes oral medication and possible injections.

Whipworm

Whipworms live in the large intestine and are difficult to spot in a stool sample. Signs of infection may include a mucus covering at the tip of your dog's stool. These parasites are typically not serious but can cause weight loss. Treatment includes oral medication.

Coccidia, Giardia, and Spirochetes

These are not worms; they are single-celled parasites that can do much damage to your dog before you even know he is infected. These parasites can cause lasting diseases and issues for a dog and require swift treatment from a vet. Often transmitted through water, food, soil, and feces, these parasites live in unsanitary conditions.

Young puppies and older dogs are more susceptible due to their weakened immune systems. Oral medication is needed.

Heartworm

Heartworms are much more severe than other intestinal parasites. These worms are transmitted via mosquito bite and typically take anywhere from six to seven months to develop into adult heartworms, which live in your dog's heart and cause major issues. These worms can cause lung, heart, and artery damage that may be permanent.

Treatment at the earliest sign of infection is crucial and may be the difference between life and death for your Portuguese Water Dog. Early symptoms include loss of appetite, cough, fatigue, and no motivation to get moving or play. As the disease progresses, these symptoms will become more severe and include bloating and even heart failure.

Heartworms are common in the southern portion of the United States, especially around the Gulf of Mexico; however, cases have been recorded in all 50 states. Preventative medication should be started around the age of six months. Options for this preventative include topical, oral, and injection. Discuss a detailed prevention plan with your vet.

Your vet will most likely require yearly heartworm testing for your Portuguese Water Dog, even if he is on a preventative. This disease is very dangerous and difficult to treat. If your dog is diagnosed with heartworm disease, treatment can cost anywhere from $500 to $1,500, and it isn't guaranteed to work.

Vaccinations

> **"**
>
> *Your puppy lacks full immunities when it comes home. It is not safe to take your puppy to public places such as rest stops, parks, and pet stores, where there is high pet traffic. Discuss with your vet when it is safe for your puppy to visit these types of places.*
>
> JILL ROUDEBUSH
> *Maritimo Portuguese Water Dogs*
>
> **"**

Vaccinations are an important tool for keeping your Portuguese Water Dog healthy and safe from potentially life-threatening illnesses. These vaccines work by injecting the body with antigens to elicit an immune response, producing antibodies for those diseases. While your dog does not actually contract the disease after injection, the antibodies are able to form and build immunity to the disease going forward.

Distemper, adenovirus, hepatitis, parvovirus, and parainfluenza are considered the core vaccinations that every puppy should receive when nursing ends at about six weeks of age. These shots are usually given in four rounds: once at six weeks, 10 weeks, 14 weeks, and 18 weeks. Many vets prefer to administer these vaccines in one shot, called a 5-Way.

Depending on where you live and your dog's risk factors, your vet may also recommend vaccinations for Bordetella and Leptospirosis.

The rabies vaccine is required legally in most areas and is administered separately, no sooner than 12 weeks of age. This vaccine must be administered every one to three years.

While these vaccines are mostly safe and effective, negative reactions can occur. Allergic reactions to vaccinations can cause hives, swelling, vomiting, and fever. Notify your vet immediately of any negative reactions, even if mild. The symptoms could worsen after the next round of shots.

Oftentimes, but not always, vaccinations are required to access many dog-related facilities. These may include kennels for boarding or day care, groomers, and, sometimes, training facilities. Be sure to keep access to vaccination records in case you need to show proof.

Common Allergens

Just like humans can have allergies to common foods and things in the environment, your Portuguese Water Dog can too. According to Cheryl W. Hoofnagle with Blue Run Portuguese Water Dogs in Maryland, "About 20% of Portuguese Water Dogs have allergies. Many allergies are to inhalants (grasses, pollens, etc.), but when it is a food allergy, it almost always is an allergy to chicken or other fowl in the food. Allergic dogs scratch and lick their paws."

If you suspect your dog may have allergies, discuss options for treatment with your vet.

Common Diseases and Conditions

Bone and Joint Disease – A Portuguese Water Dog can suffer from several bone and joint issues. Hip and elbow dysplasia are both commonly inherited diseases. This is when the joints develop improperly, which can lead to painful rubbing, arthritis, and even lameness. If you notice your dog moving painfully or getting up slower than usual, have him checked for dysplasia. The sooner it is caught, the more successful treatment is, typically.

Usually not diagnosed until two years of age, hip dysplasia is not a life-threatening disease, but it can greatly reduce the quality of a dog's life. Sometimes, hip dysplasia can be managed with drugs, weight control, and monitored exercise. X-rays can determine the severity of the dysplasia. In severe situations, surgery may be the best option to give your Portie the fullest life possible.

Addison's Disease

Addison's disease, also known as hypoadrenocorticism, results in decreased hormone production from the outer cortex of the adrenal gland. Symptoms of this disease are usually vague. They may include lethargy, diarrhea, vomiting, increased thirst and urination, and weight loss. Shaking episodes are also present occasionally.

If your Portuguese Water Dog is exhibiting any of these symptoms, Addison's disease should be considered. Once diagnosed, treatment involves lifelong injectable hormone replacement therapy, often accompanied by steroids. It may take a while to regulate your dog's hormone levels, so expect frequent visits to the vet for tests. Treatment for Addison's disease is typically successful, and your dog should resume a normal and healthy life if he continues treatment.

Gangliosidosis

This is a rare and fatal metabolic disorder in dogs that affects multiple body systems. According to the Portuguese Water Dog Foundation, "Puppies display neurological signs including vision loss, behavioral changes, gait abnormalities, and seizures. The lysosomes are a cellular structure that breaks down and recycles cellular waste. With storage diseases, these lysosomes malfunction and no longer break down and recycle cellular waste, resulting in organ malfunction."

The good news is, also according to the Portuguese Water Dog Foundation, genetic testing for this disease has been available since September 1999, making it possible to test parents before breeding and not produce puppies with this condition. The result of testing is the rate of carriers is now less than 1%.

Juvenile Dilated Cardiomyopathy

This is a fatal heart condition genetically inherited in Portuguese Water Dogs. According to ACOSTAR, a Portuguese Water Dog breeder in Canada, "An affected puppy will die usually between six and 27 weeks of age. Symptoms include a very rapid decline in appetite and energy level, weakness, vomiting, difficulty breathing, and a rapid heart rate. Death may occur within 12 to 24 hours of the appearance of these symptoms."

Death from juvenile dilated cardiomyopathy is typically sudden. There is no treatment or cure for this genetic condition. You should always ask a breeder if they have ever produced a puppy with juvenile dilated cardiomyopathy before purchasing from them.

Photo Courtesy of Ana Donlan

Progressive Retinal Atrophy (PRA)

This is a condition that affects the photoreceptor cells in the eyes and can lead to vision loss and blindness over time. There is no treatment or cure for PRA currently, so learning to adjust and help your dog cope with vision loss can help him lead the best life possible.

Alopecia

Alopecia is a harmless skin condition that causes patchy hair loss and growth. This condition can be seasonal for some dogs but not for others. Aside from physical appearance, alopecia doesn't cause other health issues, so it does not require treatment.

Prevention

Genetic testing is the best method of prevention for serious conditions and diseases such as those mentioned above. This goes back to the importance of finding a reputable breeder who is dedicated to breeding only the best and healthiest Portuguese Water Dogs. Refer to Chapter 2 for tips on what to look for in a good breeder.

Holistic Alternatives and Supplements

Whether you are looking for a way to treat your sick Portie or you're just seeking preventative care, a healthy dog begins with a healthy lifestyle. This includes proper diet and exercise. Holistic alternatives are also becoming more and more common. These alternatives have been used for centuries and are getting some attention back in the spotlight as of late.

Acupuncture

Acupuncture involves pricking the skin with needles. It has notable benefits for managing pain and increasing circulation. Supporting overall wellness, acupuncture can aid in the treatment of hip dysplasia, allergies, gastrointestinal problems, and pain due to cancer treatments.

Acupuncture causes no pain and is shown to have a calming effect in pets. Though this is a promising alternative to medications, you should always consult your veterinarian before beginning any treatment. Acupuncture should only be performed by a certified acupuncturist.

Herbs

Not all herbs are safe for your Portuguese Water Dog. Some can interact with medications your dog may be taking and have unintentional ill effects. Discuss all herbs with your vet before adding them to your dog's diet or lifestyle. Some commonly used herbs include:

Goldenseal

Anti-inflammatory and antibacterial, goldenseal can be used externally on bodily infections or as an eyewash for infections or conjunctivitis. It can be taken internally at the first sign of kennel cough or digestive issues and can also be beneficial in the treatment of tapeworms and giardia. Goldenseal should not be used for too long as it can cause stress on the liver.

Milk Thistle

Milk thistle may protect against liver damage. If your dog is on any medication that can damage his liver, discuss adding milk thistle to his regimen with your vet.

Ginger

Just as with people, ginger is an effective tool for treating nausea and cardiovascular conditions in dogs. Ginger has cardiotonic effects and can promote the functionality of the heart.

Chamomile

Another herb that aids digestion, relieves muscle spasms, and reduces inflammation, chamomile is a great option for treating chronic bowel and gas disorders and can also ease your dog's anxiety.

Licorice

Licorice root is a fast-acting anti-inflammatory that can be used to treat arthritis and other inflammatory diseases. It has been shown to enhance the efficacy of other herbs, so it is often combined with others as a part of a treatment plan.

CBD Oil

The AKC's website states, "Currently, there has been no formal study on how CBD affects dogs. What scientists do know is that cannabinoids interact with the endocannabinoid receptors located in the central and peripheral nervous systems, which help maintain balance in the body and keep it in a normal healthy state."

CBD oil, also known as cannabidiol, is thought to treat pain and help control seizures in dogs. Anecdotal evidence also shows that CBD oil may have anti-inflammatory, anti-cancer, anti-anxiety, and cardiac benefits. Discuss with your vet the option of adding a CBD supplement to your dog's diet.

This is not a comprehensive list of herbs used for dogs. If you want your dog to experience the benefits of herbal remedies but can't source the herbs yourself, there are many premade solutions and tinctures available, conveniently packaged and mixed with directions. This can help ensure you are using the herb correctly.

Only use herbs and supplements from reputable and trustworthy companies. Beware of cheaper products that may contain synthetics. And always consult your vet before beginning any herbal treatment for your Portie.

Pet Insurance

Pet insurance is an option for your Portuguese Water Dog; however, this option needs to be carefully researched. While pet insurance can protect you in the event any conditions arise, it can also be costly and unbeneficial. Each company offers different coverage, so be sure to read the fine print and understand any exclusions; there is almost always an annual deductible you must meet before insurance will cover any costs. Even after that is met, many policies only cover 80%, with wellness exams and vaccines not included.

Rates will depend on your dog's age and condition. Unless something considerable comes up, it may be more affordable to simply pay out of pocket for services. Ask your vet what pet insurance he recommends, and go from there.

CHAPTER 14

Nutrition

> "
>
> *When considering a dog food brand, look at the first five ingredients—they make up the bulk of what your dog is eating. Check the fiber content. Higher fiber generally means more pooping. I never support grain-free diets. There is a connection to heart issues with them, and dogs are herbivores as well as carnivores. Give them a quality, well-rounded diet.*
>
> ROBIN L. BURMEISTER
> *Windward Portuguese Water Dogs*
>
> "

Why Quality Food Matters

When it comes to feeding ourselves, we know that there are some foods that are better for us than others. For the sake of our health, we do our best to eat a balanced diet and avoid processed foods with harmful additives. These same rules apply when it comes to feeding our dogs. Just like humans, dogs need a certain balance of protein, fats, carbohydrates, vitamins, and minerals to keep their bodies going.

All commercial dog foods have been tested rigorously and are required to meet minimum nutritional requirements. Although this is true, minimum requirements are not what is best for your dog's long-term health. Feeding your Portie low-quality dog food is the equivalent of feeding him junk food. Choosing a dog food that is made with the best ingredients and does not include preservatives and additives will help your dog function at his optimal level, potentially protecting against disease.

According to Dr. Hugh Stevenson, a veterinarian in Ontario, Canada, for over twenty years, symptoms of poor nutrition include a dull, thin

coat, poor-quality footpads (which can crack or bleed), weight problems, excess stool and gas, and passing undigested grain particles in feces. Quality dog nutrition leads to a lustrous coat, healthy skin and weight, and less stool due to more of the food being digestible. For the sake of your Portuguese Water Dog, choose the highest quality food you have available to you, as this will be of immense benefit for years to come. Below we will discuss different dog food options you may consider for your Portie.

> **"**
>
> *Feed your PWD a high-quality pet food. Foods at grocery stores and Walmart are not a healthy choice for your dog. Meat should be the number-one ingredient in your dog food.*
>
> JILL ROUDEBUSH
> *Maritimo Portuguese Water Dogs*
> **"**

Types of Commercial Dog Foods

There are many dog foods that claim to be the best, healthiest, and most complete. It can be both overwhelming and confusing. Should you buy dry kibble? Canned wet food? Each contains a different list of ingredients and promises on the label. So how do you really know what you're getting?

The first choice you will have to make is whether to feed your dog dry kibble or wet food. Each choice comes with its own set of positives and negatives.

Wet Dog Food

Wet dog food has a very strong smell. This may be a positive for a dog who is particularly picky or doesn't have much interest in eating, as the strong scent may entice him to eat. It could also be a negative if you don't want to smell the food in your home every time you feed your Portie. Wet food also helps with hydration if you have a dog that doesn't

drink as much as he should, but it spoils quickly after opening. If your dog doesn't finish his food promptly, you'll need to store the rest in the refrigerator. Canned food can also be a bit messier to eat, getting caught in a Portie's beard and hair.

Dry Dog Food

Dry dog food doesn't spoil when left out. This is beneficial for a dog who may like to come back to his food and finish later. Dry dog food also doesn't have much of a smell, so it can sit out without anyone noticing. Some dry kibble is formulated to help clean your dog's teeth while he chews, although some experts say the added grains in certain dry foods contribute to tooth decay.

Whichever type of food you choose for your dog, it's important to remember that both canned food and kibble exist in low-quality forms. Low-quality brands include cheap fillers, artificial colors, flavors, and pre-servatives and should be avoided.

Ingredients to Avoid

It can be confusing reading the ingredient list on a dog food label. Companies that produce low-quality dog food use vague terms and scientific words to try and make you think the product contains quality, wholesome ingredients when it may not. Below is a list of key ingredients to avoid when searching for the best commercial dog food for your Portie.

BHA/BHT

Studies are not conclusive, but these chemical preservatives have been linked to hyperactivity and cancer. Used to preserve fats in human food and pet food, BHA and BHT have been banned in some countries but are still allowed in the United States, Canada, and Europe. Until conclusive evidence proves these preservatives are safe, it's best to avoid them altogether.

Meat, Meat Meal, or Rendered Fat

Any time you see a vague, nonspecific term such as "meat" or "meat meal," you can bet these are the lowest-quality ingredients allowed. These ingredients are leftovers from slaughterhouses—the parts humans won't eat. It can also include leftover, expired meats from the grocery store and diseased or dying livestock. Instead, look for specific meat terms you recognize, such as turkey, beef, salmon, lamb, or chicken.

If your dog food contains salmon or salmon meal, make sure it's labeled "wild-caught." Farm-raised salmon is less nutrient-dense than its wild counterpart because of the unnatural diet the fish are fed and has been found to potentially contain more contaminants.

HEALTH ALERT!

Obesity Woes

As an exceptionally athletic breed, Portuguese Water Dogs need plenty of exercise and a good diet to maintain their optimum weight. PWDs are prone to obesity if their exercise and nutrition needs aren't appropriately met. The AKC suggests that adult PWDs should weigh between 35 and 60 pounds, with adult females on the lower end of the spectrum and adult males at the upper end. Obesity can exacerbate hip dysplasia in PWDs, so check with your veterinarian to find your dog's ideal weight.

Photo Courtesy of
Chris and Jon Zombek

Nitrites and Nitrates

Chemical additives used to preserve freshness and extend the shelf life of meat products, nitrates and nitrites are found in human and dog food. Sodium nitrite can be toxic to your dog in high doses and has been linked to cancer.

Soy

Soy is cheap and readily available. Dog food manufacturers may use it as an inexpensive way to boost the protein percentage of the food, but it can be difficult for your dog to digest and can cause gastrointestinal upset.

Other ingredients to avoid include meat by-products, sodium hexametaphosphate, food dyes, carrageenan, taurine, cellulose, artificial flavors, and corn syrup. Dog food manufacturers dedicated to producing a quality, superior dog food will not use these red-flag ingredients. Though they can be a bit more expensive, the cost will be well worth it and may even save you money in vet bills in the long term by nourishing your dog properly.

There has been a recent trend in grain-free dog food. Some claim that because wolves in the wild don't consume more than a trace amount of grains, domesticated dogs shouldn't either. The truth is that dogs are not genetically identical to wolves, and they have adapted to utilize grains effectively.

Grain-free dog food contains other plants instead of grains. These are usually peas, lentils, potatoes, and legumes. These plant sources provide the starch to make the kibble and supply an added protein boost, allowing the manufacturer to cut back on the more expensive animal proteins. This can lead to a depletion of the amino acid taurine. Taurine is found in animal proteins but not in plant proteins, and the FDA has linked a lack of taurine to a rise in cardiomyopathy in dogs who have been fed a grain-free diet. It is best to discuss with your vet what food is best for your Portie before jumping on the grain-free trend.

> 66
>
> *We prefer PWDs be fed a fish-based protein diet. We do not encourage raw diets.*
>
> CATHERINE M. DUGAN
> *Aviator Kennels*
>
> 99

Homemade Dog Foods

The only way to know exactly what your Portie is eating is to take matters into your own hands and prepare homemade dog food. If you have the time and the resources to do this, homemade dog food can be a wonderful source of balanced whole foods for your dog, providing him with optimal nutrition without the fillers and preservatives present in commercial foods. In addition, food cooked at home contains more nutrients than processed food. This is because the high temperature used during processing causes a significant loss of nutrients.

Many homemade dog food recipes can be found online, but it's very important that you discuss specific recipes with your vet to be sure they provide your dog with all of the nutrients he needs. Individual breeds and even dogs of the same breed can have different nutritional needs. When making your dog's food yourself, it's important to get a professional opinion regarding ingredients and serving size.

Table Food – What is Good and What is Bad?

If you are keen on feeding your Portie scraps from your table, it is important you know what he can and cannot have off your plate. In Chapter 3, we covered a list of foods that would be dangerous for your dog to eat. You may want to refresh your memory before reading this list of foods that are okay for your dog to eat.

Remember, feeding your dog directly from the table can quickly form bad habits such as begging. This may be cute the first time, but it may get old fast when you want to enjoy a meal in peace.

There are a number of things you can safely share with your dog from your kitchen as a special treat or snack, but remember that these should be given in moderation so that they don't upset the balance of your dog's nutrition. None of these items should be heavily seasoned, as this may cause an upset stomach.

- White and brown rice
- Cooked eggs
- Oatmeal
- Carrots
- Cheese

- Peanut butter (without xylitol)
- Berries
- Green beans
- Seedless watermelon
- Bananas

- Peas
- Pineapple
- Apples
- Broccoli
- Potatoes

This is not a comprehensive list, and food sensitivities can differ from dog to dog, so consult your veterinarian if you think your dog may have a food allergy or sensitivity.

Weight Management

An overweight Portuguese Water Dog should be dealt with immediately. Being overweight can significantly impact his quality of life in the short term, but especially as he ages. Both diet and exercise should be evaluated to see where the problem may be originating.

Begin by implementing a more active routine. Your Portie should be engaging in physical activity every single day, and if he is not, his weight may suffer. Consult Chapter 9 for ideas to make exercise fun for you and your dog. If your Portie has not been exercising, ease him into a regular routine and increase the intensity as his body allows.

Also, consider where your dog is getting his nutrition. Is he eating a quality commercial food? Low-quality foods contain filler ingredients that will fill your dog up temporarily but don't provide adequate nutrients. Your dog may end up eating more of these foods to make up for the lack of nutrition, causing weight issues. If you prepare homemade dog food for your pup, you may need to go back to the vet or nutritionist to reevaluate ingredients and portion sizes.

Is your Portie eating too many snacks outside mealtime? You may love sharing a snack or two throughout the day, but if it is negatively impacting his weight and health, you should keep the snacking to a minimum. Remember, moderation is key.

If you can't get your dog's weight under control by limiting snacks and providing a quality commercial food, discuss options with your vet. He or she may suggest a weight management food. These foods feature higher than average protein, lower than average fat, and fewer calories. These foods are formulated for adult dogs only and should never be given to a puppy. Remember to read food labels and choose a food made with high-quality ingredients.

CHAPTER 15

Dealing with Unwanted Behaviors

What is Considered Bad Behavior?

No two dogs are alike, even within the same breed! Just like humans, each dog has a unique personality that you must get to know. Everyone wants a well-trained, obedient dog that will sit quietly waiting for the next command, but even successful training won't keep a spunky dog from being spunky. Just like humans, dogs can exhibit behaviors that are annoying at times, but that doesn't necessarily mean they are bad. So, when it comes to bad habits and behaviors, what is considered "bad?"

Barking

Barking is as natural for your dog as speaking is to you and should never be considered bad behavior. If your dog is extra chatty and you find this to be an annoyance, there are measures you can take to correct the behavior.

First, determine if there is a reason for the behavior. Is there a direct cause for the barking, such as your Portie seeing other people or dogs? If so, socializing your Portie may go a long way in quelching that behavior.

If the problem is more sporadic and inconsistent, consider

whether your Portie may simply be trying to get your attention. Are you spending enough intentional time with your dog? Is he getting enough social and physical engagement throughout the day? Barking may be your Portie's method of getting attention.

Digging

Much like chasing, digging is a natural behavior and may involve rolling around in the freshly disturbed dirt. This is not bad behavior. But it can become annoying and may be curbed with stricter supervision and obedience training.

Chasing

The Portuguese Water Dog has a low prey drive and typically does well with smaller animals and pets. However, chasing may still be a problem for a spunky, playful Portie. While this behavior can be annoying and dangerous, it should never be treated as "bad" behavior. Your dog is only doing what comes naturally to him. Obedience training can help the issue, but it may not ever stop it completely.

Though not bad behavior, chasing can be a dangerous habit, especially in a city with cars and other hidden dangers. Unless you can be sure he won't chase a neighborhood cat or a skateboarder riding down the street, you will need to keep your Portie leashed or contained behind a fence the entire time he is out.

Leash Pulling

This is a direct result of improper or inadequate training and is not bad behavior. Teach your dog the proper way to walk on a leash with the help of a trainer, and this annoyance can be eliminated altogether.

Other unwanted behaviors that are not "bad" include chewing up toys or shoes, begging or stealing food, jumping on people, getting on furniture, and eating poop. All of these behaviors can be a nuisance but are typically not evidence of a poorly behaved dog.

Aggression

Behavior that should always be considered "bad" is any form of unprovoked aggression. This could be vicious growling, biting, lunging,

FUN FACT
Unique Feet

PWDs are notoriously prolific swimmers, but did you know they have a genetic advantage in this department? Webbed paws are the Portuguese Water Dog's secret weapon, propelling them through the water remarkably efficiently. Most dogs have some degree of webbing between their toes, but this advantageous feature is more pronounced in PWDs than in most other breeds. In addition to their unique toes, PWDs sport a waterproof coat and athletic build for increased endurance.

or snarling. These behaviors are unacceptable, and if not dealt with immediately, they can result in serious injury or death for your dog or the object of his aggression. This includes food or possession aggression. There may be a root issue or trigger that you are not aware of, so consult a professional trainer or animal psychologist promptly if you are dealing with these truly bad and dangerous dog behaviors.

Getting to the Root of the Problem

The first step to eliminating unwanted behavior is to find out why your Portie is doing it. Learning why he's exhibiting a certain behavior can make correcting or redirecting the problem much easier for you and your dog.

Instinctual

Many times, unwanted behavior stems from instinct. If this is the case, the behavior will be more challenging to stop. Consult a professional trainer for help, but also try to redirect the instinctual behavior in a positive way.

Lack of Training

Most of the unwanted behaviors on this list actually begin with a lack of proper training. Time spent consistently training your dog is the best way to correct these annoyances. See chapter 10 for more training tips and how to get started.

Photo Courtesy of
Lynn Gaylord

Past Trauma

If you are dealing with aggression issues, consider any traumas in your dog's past, especially if you adopted him later in his life. These issues need to be dealt with by a trained professional, so seek help immediately.

How to Correct Your Dog

Punishment is not an effective way to correct unwanted behaviors in your dog. Your Portuguese Water Dog will want to please you with his actions, so if he's doing something undesirable, it's because he isn't sure what is right. Correct him by showing him what you want him to do and not what you don't want him to do. Reward him for positive behavior, and he is sure to catch on quickly.

When to Call a Professional

Usually, unwanted behaviors in dogs are just annoyances and not so much "bad." However, even behaviors that come naturally to your dog can become dangerous if left unchecked. Digging holes in the yard is irritating, but it becomes a safety issue if your Portie begins digging those holes under the fence. Chewing can be upsetting when your favorite pair of sandals fall victim, but it is not inherently dangerous. On the other hand, chewing on an electrical cord can be deadly.

If your attempts to redirect the behavior have been unsuccessful, seek a professional trainer's help. They have seen these issues time and time again and will have the resources and experience to find a solution that works for both you and your dog. The longer you wait, the harder these bad habits will be to break.

CHAPTER 16

Caring for Your Senior Portuguese Water Dog

> *Keeping your PWD active and lean will help enrich its later years.*
>
> CHRISTIE KELLO
> *Windward Portuguese Water Dogs*

Caring for your aging Portie is a responsibility all owners will face at some point. Much like humans, dogs typically require more medical care and face more ailments as they grow into their senior years. Conditions such as arthritis, cognitive dysfunction, cataracts, hearing loss, incontinence, and an inability to regulate body temperature become typical.

According to the AKC, the Portuguese Water Dog has an average life span of 11 to 13 years. This means your Portie will likely enter the senior stage around year seven or eight. Not all dogs reach this stage at the same time, however, and many can live comfortable and happy lives for years. This chapter will discuss potential issues you may face with your aging dog and help you navigate the difficult end-of-life decisions when the time comes.

Common Old-Age Ailments

> **"**
>
> *Be patient with your dog if it is slow to react when you ask something of it. Don't get frustrated when you call your dog and it ignores you. Chances are your dog has lost some of its hearing. Old dogs tend to get cataracts in their later years. Get a senior blood panel when your dog is seven or eight years of age. Have the thyroid checked to be sure that it is normal. I think the biggest thing to remember when your dog is older is to be more loving and patient with it.*
>
> JILL ROUDEBUSH
> *Maritimo Portuguese Water Dogs*
>
> **"**

Arthritis

Osteoarthritis is a degenerative joint disease where the bones of a joint rub against each other due to the deterioration of the cartilage between them. This deterioration can cause severe pain, stiffness, and limited mobility. Osteoarthritis cannot be cured, but it can be treated with medication and supplements to slow the progression of the disease and treat symptoms.

Cataracts

Cataracts cause a dog to have blurry vision by creating an opacity in the normally clear lens. If your senior dog develops cataracts, have your vet monitor him closely for worsening symptoms. When left untreated, cataracts can sometimes lead to blindness. While this is not a death sentence for your Portie, it would take a major life adjustment for you and him. Many blind dogs live happy and healthy lives otherwise!

Cognitive Dysfunction

Senior dogs are susceptible to dementia, just like humans are. If you notice your dog forgetting something he does often or acting unusually out of his normal routine, discuss options with your vet for helping improve his quality of life. If your dog experiences these symptoms, try to ease his frustration and confusion by making everyday tasks simpler for him. This could mean putting his food and water in a more visible place in the house, leading him outside more often or using a puppy pad to avoid accidents, and keeping his toys and belongings easily accessible.

Just like with humans, dogs with cognitive dysfunction can benefit greatly from mental stimulation. Continue to review and practice basic commands, such as sit and stay with your senior dog or play a basic game of hide-and-seek with a toy. These activities can help to slow the worsening of this condition and can even help improve memory.

Hearing Loss

Hearing loss is common for old dogs. While many will lose some degree of hearing, they may not go completely deaf. Signs of hearing loss include a sudden lack of obedience, increased startle reaction, and excessive barking.

If your dog experiences hearing loss, you may need to find another form of communication. Teach your dog hand signals at the first sign of hearing loss so that if he loses his hearing completely, you can still communicate commands. It may also be helpful to keep a flashlight handy to signal for his attention.

Basic Senior Dog Care

> ❝
> *Do annual blood work and be especially observant of any changes in behavior. Changes in drinking, eating, stools, weight, or desire to go out are all possible warning signs. Dogs are not complainers. It's our job to observe and interpret their behaviors.*
>
> MARLENE NICEWANDER
> *Cove's End Portuguese Water Dogs*
> ❞

Photo Courtesy of Nicole Sendar

Care for a senior dog should be focused on keeping him comfortable and happy. Like people, senior dogs have trouble regulating their body temperature. Be sure to provide your dog with extra warmth on a cold day, and make sure he stays cool on a hot day.

Special accommodations may need to be made to make life more comfortable for your aging dog. For example, if your dog has arthritis, he may benefit from a bed made specifically to help with stiffness. If you have stairs, you may also need to consider keeping all your dog's things on the lowest level of your home so he doesn't need to climb the stairs. A stepstool to help him reach his favorite spot on the couch may also be nice.

As a dog ages, energy levels usually decline along with stamina. It's important that you still give your aging Portie regular, gentle exercise to keep him in shape. Obesity can be a problem in older dogs, who typically move around less, and it can exacerbate other age-related ailments such as arthritis and heart conditions. If obesity becomes a problem despite regular exercise, discuss options with your veterinarian. He or she may suggest switching to a different food or changing portion size.

Your senior dog will probably need to see the vet more in his last years. The AAHA (American Animal Hospital Association) recommends that you take your senior dog to the vet at least once every six months for a check-up. These regular vet visits can help you catch any conditions early and allow for more prompt treatment, potentially leading to a better quality of life.

Illness and Injury Prevention

Both illness and injury are more difficult to overcome for an older dog. The best way to prevent illness and injury is to know your Portie's limits. Exercise should be adapted to meet your aging dog's physical needs, but it should never be stopped altogether. Exercise is extremely important for an older dog, just as it was when he was younger.

Because your aging dog is more prone to injury, exercise should be done more slowly and with little to no impact on joints. This means no jumping, climbing, or walking at an incline for a prolonged period.

Instead, try a slow, leisurely walk or a swim. If you notice your dog limping after exercise, dial it back and take it easier to avoid injury or pain.

Patti McKnight from McKnights PWDs in Illinois says, "A Portuguese Water Dog can be 12 to 13 years old and still be very active. But watch your dog. It will let you know when it is tired and has had enough. Let common sense be your guide."

Also, staying up to date on your Portuguese Water Dog's vaccinations and medications, including flea and tick preventatives, can go a long way in helping to keep him well in his later years. If your elderly dog does become ill, he is more likely to suffer life-threatening complications than his younger counterparts. A case of kennel cough may be no big deal for a young dog, but it could quickly lead to a dangerous case of pneumonia for a senior dog.

Ultimately, you will need to be patient with your Portie as he ages and remember that this is a normal life progression. Adjustments will need to be made and lifestyle changes implemented. Try to enjoy the later years with your dog and learn to slow down with him. Robin L. Burmeister from Windward Portuguese Water Dogs in Ohio says, "Take them for walks and car rides. Just because they may be less active doesn't mean they don't crave your companionship. They need your reassurance that they are still loved more than ever."

Supplements and Nutrition

Good nutrition is still key to keeping your senior dog in his best shape and condition, even in the later years. Quality of life and severity of conditions is directly affected by nutrition, including supplements. Though there are several supplements on the market formulated for senior dogs, always ask your vet before adding anything to your dog's diet, as there is a potential for side effects and drug interactions.

Here is a list of the most common supplements used for senior dogs.

Glucosamine and Chondroitin

Two supplements often paired together to combat osteoarthritis, glucosamine and chondroitin, have been found to be therapeutic in the treatment of canine arthritis. These compounds are found naturally in cartilage and are made by the body.

When looking for a glucosamine and chondroitin supplement, look for highly reputable brands that source all their ingredients from the United States. Imported glucosamine has been found to contain many contaminants, including lead, especially when sourced from China. Since the FDA does not regulate supplements, the only way to know if you are getting a quality product is to be vigilant and diligent in your research. Even popular pet store brands that say "made in the USA" can include ingredients sourced from China.

Omega- 3 Fatty Acids

Omega-3 fatty acids like DHA and EPA have been shown to be beneficial to the brain, potentially improving cognitive function in old age, and they may even give your dog's immune system a boost. According to the AKC, "The addition of omega-3 to the diet may [also] help reduce inflammation and can promote cell membrane health."

Antioxidants

Including an extra source of antioxidants in your senior Portie's diet can be beneficial as well. You can do this by purchasing a supplement or by simply allowing your dog to snack on high-antioxidant fruits such as berries and apples.

Probiotics

Probiotics help maintain healthy bacteria in the gut, the place where up to 80% of a dog's immune defenses reside. This can improve immune function and help your senior dog fight off illness and disease more efficiently.

FUN FACT
Canine Cancer

Portuguese Water Dogs have an average life span of 12 to 15 years and are a generally hardy breed. Unfortunately, the leading cause of death for PWDs is hemangiosarcoma (HSA), followed by lymphoma or lymphosarcoma, cancer affecting the lymph nodes. Based on a 2014 health survey, the PWDCA found that 42% of the reported deaths for this breed were caused by cancer. Therefore, the PWDCA continues to support research into canine cancer treatments. Cancer treatments vary based on your dog's diagnosis and should be discussed with an oncologist.

When It's Time to Say Goodbye

No Portuguese Water Dog owner wants to face saying goodbye to a loyal companion and friend. Understanding when this time is near and preparing for the end is one of the most difficult times in pet ownership, but it is ultimately our responsibility as owners and caretakers to be loving and selfless as a dog nears this time.

When the time comes, and your Portie may be experiencing more pain than happiness, it may be time to consider humanely ending his life to relieve him from the pain of his final days. This decision is never made easily and can lead to an array of emotions for the owner, including sorrow, guilt, and oftentimes, second thoughts. These emotions are normal and will likely be there no matter how many times you are faced with a dog's end-of-life decisions.

How Will You Know When the Time Is Right?

You and your Portuguese Water Dog have formed a bond over your years together that only you can know the depth of. Therefore, you are the best and only one who should make the final call. If you have a gut feeling that your Portie has made a sharp decline in health and is hurting more than he is not, the time may be right to make the call. A few telltale signs that death is imminent are extreme lethargy, lack of interest in anything, loss of coordination, incontinence, and not eating or drinking.

Only you and your dog will know when this time is. Your dog has trusted you with his life thus far, and he trusts you with it now. If you believe putting him down humanely will end his suffering, speak to your vet and discuss euthanasia.

Once you have made the decision that the time has come to humanely end your dog's suffering, know that second thoughts are normal. This decision will always be hard. Don't second guess the decision that is best for your dog just because it's hard for you. Grieving over this decision, even before it has happened, is natural and normal. Talk to a trusted therapist, friend, or family member to help you cope during this difficult time.

Once you have made the decision, and if the vet agrees death is inevitable, the process happens fairly quickly. The point is to end your dog's suffering, so there is no sense in putting it off for a few days.

The Euthanasia Process

Before you take your dog to the vet, call anyone who may want to say goodbye to him. Some even choose to host a special day with their dog, feeding him all his favorite foods and taking him to see his favorite spots one last time. If you choose to do this, make it a happy and relaxed day for your dog.

When it's time, you will have the option to be present when the vet performs the procedure. Although it may be hard for you to watch your dog die, know that it will bring your dog comfort and peace in his last moments if you are there with him, holding him and comforting him.

During the procedure, your vet will administer a solution, typically phenobarbital, intravenously. The solution is usually thick with a blue, pink, or purple tint. The vet may inject it directly into a vein or into an intravenous catheter. Once the solution is injected, it will quickly travel through your dog's body, causing him to lose consciousness within just a few seconds. Your Portie will feel no pain. Breathing will slow and then stop altogether. Cardiac arrest will occur and cause death within 30 seconds of the injection.

Your vet will check for signs of life and will most likely step out of the room for a few moments to give you time to say a final goodbye. Your vet and his office staff have been through this before and will understand the emotional weight of the situation for you. They should provide you with privacy and be a source of comfort if needed. Be sure to make payments and after-death arrangements beforehand so you don't have to deal with it after—while you are grieving.

Your dog's body may still move after death, so don't be alarmed if you see twitching. He may also release bodily fluids, and this is also normal. When you are ready, leave your dog and allow the vet to proceed with his remains.

*Photo Courtesy of
Jon Zombek*

Making Final Arrangements

Cremation is a common choice for pet owners facing the death of a beloved dog. It is more affordable than a cemetery plot and allows you to keep your dog close to you via his ashes if you choose to do so. If you have chosen to have your dog cremated, your vet will coordinate with a cremation service and notify you when his ashes are ready.

If you are taking your deceased dog home for burial, the vet will place your dog's remains in a container and will typically carry it out to the car for you. Depending on where you live, burying your dog at home may or may not be legal. Check local laws ahead of time.

Even if it is legal, burying your dog at home may not be the best idea. Wild animals may attempt to dig up your Portie's remains, flood waters can cause his body to resurface, and even groundwater contamination is possible. If you want to have a memorial at your home, consider spreading his ashes there and placing a memorial stone instead of a burial.

A pet cemetery is another option for a final resting place for your Portuguese Water Dog. This is a graveyard designated just for pets. The service is not cheap, however. A plot can cost around $400 to $600, and that doesn't include the cost of the casket. While it is pricey, it is a beautiful place for your Portie to remain among other beloved pets gone before.

Whichever you choose, once you leave the vet's office, be prepared to grieve your loyal and loving Portuguese Water Dog. Grieving the loss of a pet is serious and you should seek professional help if you are struggling. Just remember, the love and bond you and your Portie shared is not lost. It remains in your heart and memories forever.